AZORES CRUISING GUIDE

Editor
Gwenda Cornell

Technical Editor
Ivan Cornell

Photographs
Jimmy Cornell

Maps
Maggie Nelson

Publisher
Jimmy Cornell

World Cruising Publications
1993

First Edition 1993
Published by World Cruising Publications
P.O. Box 165, London, England WC1B 3XA
Tel. (0)71 405 9905 Fax (0)71 831 0161

© World Cruising Publications
ISBN 0 9517486 2 9 Azores Cruising Guide (pbk)

Printed in Britain by Alpine Press
Station Road, Kings Langley, Herts
WD4 8LF

This guide has been prepared with the best information available at the time of writing. The editors and publisher disclaim all liability for any errors and omissions. This guide should not be used for navigational purposes, and must be used in conjunction with the relevant charts, pilots and sailing directions for the Azores.

All rights reserved. No part of this publication may be reproduced, stored or transmitted in any forms or by any means, without the prior permission of the publishers.

ACKNOWLEDGMENTS

This book could not have been produced without the generous help of the Secretaria Regional do Turismo, led by the Secretary for Tourism Eugenio Leal and the Director of Tourism Alberto Pereira. We are particularly grateful to Mrs Conceição Macedo for her steadfast support over the years, first with the transatlantic rallies from the Caribbean and now with this guide. Sincere thanks are also due to our old friend João Carlos Fraga, whose patience we have taxed on many occasions and who never fails to answer our many questions promptly.

The publisher wishes to thank the following people, who have contributed to this guide in various ways.

Santa Maria: Alberto Costa, Jorge Boutelho, Mario Jorge Moura, Maria José da Mota Cabral.
São Miguel: Luis Mota, Mario Sousa Teixeria, João José Fernandes, Manuel Romualdo da Silva, Fernando Sousa Henriques, Conceição Amaral.
Terceira: Carlos Manuel Fragoso.
Graciosa: Luis Reis, Valdemar Clarimon.
São Jorge: Frederico Maciel.
Pico: Armando Castro.
Faial: Renato Leal, Angelo Andrade, Luis Morais, José Lobão, Eduardo Elias da Silva, Helder Azevedo Castro, Joseph Franck.
Corvo: Dr João Cardigos dos Reis, Orlando Silva, Susana Fraga Silva.
Flores: José Maria Silva, António Francisco Melo.

Cover: Cruising yachts sailing past Pico (Photo Jimmy Cornell)

•TABLE OF CONTENTS•

Introduction 7
    History 7
    Economy 9
    Festivals 9
    Getting There 10
    Getting Away 13
    Weather 16
    Around the Islands 18
    Port Facilities 20
    General Information 21
    VHF Radio Stations 24
    Entry Procedure 25

Santa Maria 27
    Navigation 28
    Lights 30
    Vila do Porto 30
    Anjos 32
    São Lourenço, Porto da Maia, Praia Formosa 33

São Miguel 34
    Navigation, ... 35
    Lights 36
    Ponta Delgada 36
    Lagoa 42
    Caloura, Galera, Porto Caloura 43
    Vila Franca do Campo 44
    Ribeira Quente, Povoação 45
    Praia do Lombo Gordo, Nordeste, Porto Formoso, Praia dos Moinhos, Santa Iria, Ribeira Grande, Rabo do Peixe 46
    São Vicente, Capelas, Mosteiro, Candelaria 47

Terceira 48
    Navigation 49
    Lights 50
    Angra do Heroísmo 50
    Porto Judeu, Baia de Salga 54
    Porto Novo, Porto de São Fernando .. 55
    Porto Martins, Praia da Vitória 55
    Vila Nova, Ponta dos Misterios, Quatro Ribeiras, Biscoitos 56
    Ponta da Serreta, Cinco Ribeiras, Porto Negrito, Porto São Mateus, ... 57

Graciosa 58
    Navigation, Lights 59
    Santa Cruz 60
    Cais da Barra, Praia 62
    Carapacho, Folga, Porto Afonso 64

São Jorge 65
    Navigation 66
    Lights 68
    Ponta Rosais, Baia de Entre-Morros 68
    Velas 68
    Ribeira do Nabo 70
    Urzelina, Castelete, Terreiros, Fajã das Almas, Fajã Grande 71
    Calheta 72
    Topo, Ouvidor 73

Pico 74
    Navigation 75
    Lights, Madalena 76
    Porto Calhau, Porto São Mateus 79
    Porto São João, Lajes do Pico 80
    Santa Cruz das Ribeiras 81
    Calheta de Nesquim, Manhenha 82
    Santo Amaro, Prainha, Baia das Canas, São Roque 83
    São Antonio, Cachorro 84

Faial 85
    Navigation, Lights 86
    Horta 86
    Caldeira do Inferno, Porto Pim 97
    Feteira, Varadouro, Capelinho, Fajã, Praia do Almoxarife 98

Corvo 99
    Lights, Vila Nova 100
    O Boqueirão, Porto Novo, Areia, Topo 102

Flores 103
    Navigation, ... 103
    Lights, Santa Cruz 105
    East Coast 107
    Lajes 108
    Fajãzinha 110
    Fajã Grande, Ponta Delgada, São Pedro, Porto de Boqueirão 111

List of Charts 112   List of Radio Beacons 112

WELCOME TO THE AZORES

An experienced sailor with many Atlantic crossings to his credit once described the Azores as Europe's best kept cruising secret. I thought of that remark many times during a two month cruise in the Azores in the summer of 1993. During that time I visited all nine islands of the archipelago, but did not meet more than twenty other cruising yachts outside of the Horta and Ponta Delgada marinas. Although a thousand yachts called at the Azores in 1993, the vast majority left without visiting any other port outside of their first landfall. Yet, the islands have a lot more to offer. With the exception of Corvo, there is at least one good port on every island, the weather in summer is pleasant, the scenery superb, the waters clear and the Azoreans extremely welcoming.

Throughout their history, the Azores have depended on the sea for their links with the outside world and sailors have always been regarded with affection by the Azoreans. There are indeed few places in the world where yachts are welcomed with such genuine warmth. Because of the seasonal movement of

yachts, they are regarded as migratory birds and spring in Horta is heralded every year by the arrival of the first yachts from the Caribbean.

Reflecting this warmth towards sailors, the authorities have been making great efforts to provide better facilities for their floating visitors, first

by building an excellent marina in Horta and this year doing the same in the capital Ponta Delgada. Another sign that the Azores Government takes yachting seriously is this guide, which has enjoyed the wholehearted support of the Ministry of Tourism.

The main purpose of this book is to help more sailors discover the many attractions of the Azores. Keen to share that long held secret, I invited my friends David and Laurence Ambrose to cruise with us on board La Aventura. As a successful writer, David is no stranger to untangling a mystery, but the unspoilt beauty of the Azores took even him by surprise.

Jimmy Cornell

FIRST IMPRESSIONS

The idea of a group of volcanic islands somewhere out in the vastness of the Atlantic was in itself romantic enough to be intriguing. But I had little idea of what to expect apart from black sand on the beaches or extinct craters rising grandly to the sky and being lassoed by low-flying clouds. What I was not prepared for were the colours.

Far from the blacks and grays that my mind's eye had painted, I found myself in

a world of rolling green landscapes with dazzling bursts of red, blue, pink and white. There was something magical in the way that most roads were lined with dense banks of hydrangeas and wild roses, turning a simple journey into a feast for the eyes. Traffic was light, cars giving way at crossroads to a woman and horse-drawn cart; a truck slowing to make room for a farmer whose donkey had decided it didn't want to head home just yet. A pleasing mix, in other words, of old and new. Small towns where no one was a stranger, where everyone was welcomed with a simple down-to-earth hospitality. Larger towns, busy and with all the amenities you expect of the twentieth century; and yet with a sense that they had just time-slipped from the nineteenth or even earlier, their buildings unspoilt and beautifully kept up, and something in the air that acted like a cure for the usual ills of urban paranoia and pollution.

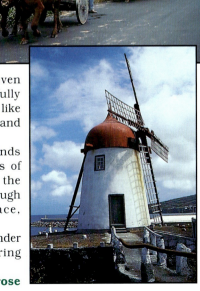

The improbability of that cluster of islands being there at all, and the unexpectedness of them when you get there, combine to give the feeling that you have somehow stepped through a secret door into an undiscovered place, somewhere in a slightly different dimension.

More than anything, they serve as a reminder that travel, even these days, can still spring surprises - including good ones.

David Ambrose

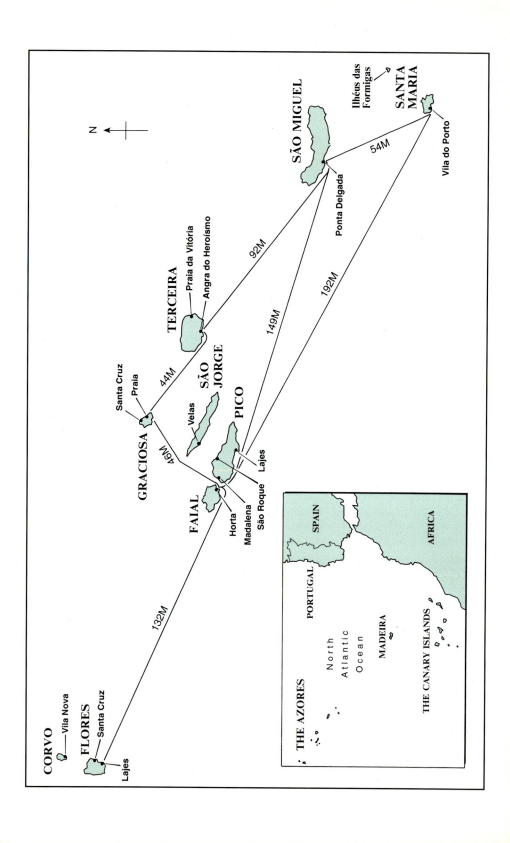

THE AZORES

Reputed to be the fabled Atlantis, the nine islands of the Azores belong truly to the Atlantic Ocean. Their nature, history and climate all derive from their position in mid-Atlantic, 900 miles off the coast of Portugal and 1800 miles from Bermuda. Located between 36° and 43° North and 25° and 31° West, the archipelago consists of nine main islands divided into three groups, the two most western islands Flores and Corvo, the central group of Faial, Pico, São Jorge, Graciosa and Terceira, and to the east the largest island São Miguel and Santa Maria. The large number of hawks seen flying over the islands, which the early settlers mistook for vultures and are called *açores* in Portuguese, have given their name to the archipelago.

Volcanic outbursts along the Atlantic seismic ridge, all the islands have a similarity in their rugged volcanic landscape of cones, lava fields and hot springs. Many of the cones have disintegrated to form vast craters called calderas, several containing beautiful lakes. Volcanic activity has often changed the face of the islands in the few hundred years of their settlement, leaving a path of destruction over towns and villages, the most recent eruption being that at Capelinhos on Faial in 1957-58. Small tremors are still registered daily and vulcanologists expect that at some point in the next 10,000 years Pico will erupt to form its own caldera.

Over the centuries the volcanic soil has become rich and fertile and aided by the mild moist climate, supports an abundant vegetation, a combination of both tropical and temperate, with forests of laurel and juniper, hedgerows of hydrangeas, lush green fields and vividly coloured flowers growing everywhere. Although similar in origin, each island has its own distinctive individuality, from flower carpeted Flores or the bubbling hot springs of the Furnas Valley in São Miguel to the perfect soaring peak of Pico, at 2,351 metres the highest mountain in Portugal.

PORTUGUESE DISCOVERY

The islands appear to have been known in ancient times, even though there was no indigenous population. Old coins found on the island of Corvo suggest that Phoenicians had passed that way. The islands appear on several Italian maps in the 14th century, but the official discovery or rather rediscovery of the islands belongs to the Portuguese.

The discovery is attributed to Diogo de Silves, who found the most eastern island Santa Maria in 1427 on a return expedition from Madeira financed by Prince Henry the Navigator to search for new lands. The rediscovery of the rest of the islands followed quickly, only the two most western ones, Flores and Corvo not being reached until 1452.

Prince Henry obtained the authority to colonise the islands and a royal charter exempting settlers from taxes meant that they were settled very quickly, both by Portuguese and also by many Flemish settlers, eager to escape from religious persecution in Flanders.

COLUMBUS CONNECTION

By the time of Columbus, the Azores had well established settlements and it is clear from various references in his journals that Columbus knew the islands, their climatic conditions and flora. It is possible that while he lived in Lisbon, Columbus sailed on one of the triangular voyages that plied regularly between Lisbon, the Azores and Galway in Ireland or Bristol in England.

The Portugese King in fact approved an expedition to discover land to the west, the navigators Dulmo and Estreito leaving Terceira in 1487, never to be heard of again. Columbus, however, had already realised that attempting to sail west from the Azores was not viable. He appears to have interpreted the winds and currents of the North Atlantic correctly and thus pioneered the optimum way to cross the Atlantic in either direction. His landing on Santa Maria in 1493, on his return voyage from the New World, established the Azores on the west to east route which is now plied by hundreds of yachts every year.

A few years after Columbus, an Azorean from Terceira, João Fernandes Labrador, sailed with Cabot's fleet and was the first to sight the land that now bears his name Labrador.

Vasco da Gama also called at Terceira in 1499 on his return from discovering the sea route to India. By 1500 the Azores were well developed and already a popular port of call for Portuguese caravels returning from Africa. The caravels preferred to sail the extra distance to the Azores so that the prevailing winds would give them a better slant on the last leg to Lisbon.

The Azores have remained closely connected with Portugal, playing an important role during the period of Spanish domination of the Atlantic. During the 16th and 17th centuries the islands became an important staging post on the routes between Europe, America and the Indies. In consequence they were prey to attacks by pirates and corsairs and many important sea battles took place in Azorean waters. When Spain occupied mainland Portugal in 1580, Dom Antonio, claimant to the Portuguese throne, fled to Terceira to organise his opposition. The islands fiercely resisted the Spanish invasion, but eventually Spain took control of all of them, and used them as a stopping off point for ships returning from South America with treasure.

INTO THE MODERN AGE

In 1640 when Portugal regained independence the islands were each ruled by an independent governor until 1766, when a central government was set up in Terceira. The latter supported the Liberals during Portugal's constitutional struggles in the early 19th century, becoming the base from which the Liberals invaded the mainland. Following the Liberal Revolution of 1832 the Azores were made a province of Portugal with three districts centred around the main ports of Horta, Angra and Ponta Delgada.

The islands were to remain an important stop for sailing ships down the centuries, the caravels being replaced by New England whalers in the 19th century, who took on many islanders as crew. Gradually the number of ships declined, to be replaced by the transatlantic flying boats in the 1930's and the offshore cruising yachts of today. In 1895 Joshua Slocum visited Horta, little knowing how many small boat sailors were to follow in his footsteps.

COMMUNICATIONS CENTRE

The Azores have played a significant role as a link in Atlantic communications, as well as provisioning sailing ships. The first transatlantic cable was laid from Horta to Nova Scotia in 1900 and the island of Faial developed as a relay point for transatlantic messages, with cable companies from several countries setting up stations there.

At the outbreak of the First World War, the British cut the four German cables, even though Portugal was neutral. The same thing happened again at the beginning of the Second World War when the British cut German and Italian cables. Once Portugal had broken relations with Germany, airbases were built on Santa Maria and Terceira, while Horta was used by the British Navy as a base. During both world wars the islands were strategically important bases for the Allies, and the US airforce still maintains a base on Terceira. The large airfield on Santa Maria was turned over to civilian use and became important for mid-Atlantic refuelling. However, with the lengthening of the range of planes and the use of satellites for telephone links, the days of the Azores as a communications relay station are over.

POLITICAL STATUS

The Azores have remained Portuguese, apart from some 50 years under Spanish rule in the early 1600's. In 1976 the Azores became an autonomous region, with their own government and assembly, allowing a certain amount of independence from the central Portuguese government and autonomy in the management of their internal affairs. Ponta Delgada on São Miguel is the capital of the autonomous region, although the government offices are spread out among three main islands: São Miguel, Faial and Terceira. The President's office is in Ponta Delgada, the Regional Assembly in Horta, while the Minister of the Republic, who represents the central government, is based in Angra do Heroísmo. The ministries, called secretariats, are shared out among the same three islands.

The local administration is in the hands of the Municipal Councils (Câmara Municipal) which are centred on the main towns. There are a quarter of a million inhabitants in the islands, of which more than half live on the largest island São Miguel. Portuguese is the main language, although English, Spanish and French are widely understood. The majority of the population are Roman Catholics.

ECONOMY

The early settlers cleared the forests for cattle raising and grain crops were also successfully grown. The agricultural economy started then still occupies many of the population today. Fishing has always been an important factor in the economy, although the traditional whaling industry has now declined. From the days when the Azores were an important centre for the whalers of New Bedford, there has always been a certain amount of emigration to the USA, and remittances from the large Azorean communities in the USA, Brazil and Bermuda play their part in the economy. Many of these emigrants still maintain homes in the Azores for their vacations. An increasing number of those who emigrated, having amassed some capital abroad, return to set up businesses or build houses for their retirement years. Tourism is rapidly expanding, but agriculture and fishing continue to be the mainstay of the local economy.

FESTIVALS

One feature of life in the Azores is the large number of festivals which take place, some secular, but most with a religious basis. Over several hundred years these religious feasts have evolved in a special way and have a unique secular flavour.

The most distinctive are the traditions associated with the Holy Ghost, Espírito Santo. The cult of the Holy Ghost was brought to the islands with the first settlers and is believed to have developed so strongly because of the volcanic eruptions and earthquakes to which the islands are prone. It was believed that the Holy Ghost guarded the population from these cataclysmic phenomena. The traditions of Espírito Santo take place on all the islands, but on Terceira they take on a particular importance.

Associated with the tradition are small chapels which contain an altar where the special crown and sceptre of the Holy Ghost are placed. The ritual is quite complex and spreads over various Sundays after Easter. Every year different people are chosen to keep the crown and on each of the Sundays, the crown is placed on the head of a chosen "emperor" and a procession takes it to the house of the next guardian. All this is accompanied by festivities at the chapels, processions, music, carpets of flowers and bullfights. Special dishes are eaten, such as Holy Ghost soup and *alcatra*, a marinated beef stew.

Also in Terceira, another tradition is a special kind of bullfighting, *corrida à corda*, which may have its origins in rituals thousands of years old. Maybe it is not coincidence that the Minoan culture associated with bull jumping originated on Crete, also an island of volcanic activity. In the *corrida á corda* the bull is let loose on the streets and any young man who wants to try his luck can make passes at the bull as it charges from one end of a village to the other. Doors and gates are barricaded while spectators crowd the walls and balconies. The bull is checked by a very long rope, the corda, which is held and controlled by a group of men, which does put the bull at a certain disadvantage. Also its horns are padded and the bull is not killed, as is also the case in the regular bullfights in the bullring at Angra do Hero°smo.

These bullfights take place in many places on various Saints' days, particularly those of St John at the end of June. Booths are set up selling food and drink, bands play, fireworks are let off and the festival atmosphere often continues into the night.

Almost every village has its own individual feast day, usually associated with the patron saint of its church. Typically this will involve a religious service followed by a procession through streets spread with a carpet of flowers, while gaily coloured quilts are hung out of the windows. The flower carpets are densely packed with flowers chosen for their colours and arranged in intricate designs. The festivities usually continue with fireworks, eating and drinking, dancing and music.

Another big festival celebrated in all the islands and which features some of the best flower carpets is that of Corpus Christi. This is particularly interesting in Madalena on Pico, where the women of the village bake a special bread, the breads being piled high in baskets decorated with flowers. After being displayed outside the church and carried in procession on the women's heads, the bread is distributed to the public.

From May to September there is always something happening on one island or another and weekends are packed with festivities. Those of particular note are the fiesta of St John in Angra do Heroísmo (mid-June), the horse calvacades of St Peter on São Miguel (29 June), the Emigrant fiesta in Lajes das Flores (mid-July) and the feast of Mary Magdalen at Madalena on Pico (22 July).

On the secular side there are many musical events, such as the Calheta festival on São Jorge in July and maritime events such as the Whalers Week in Lajes do Pico at the end of August. The majority of the yachting regattas are organised from Faial, including races to other islands to coincide with various festivities and culminating with Sea Week in Horta at the end of July.

GETTING THERE

The Azores have long been on the sailing routes of the world for boats coming from many directions, the sailing conditions of which vary considerably and will be dealt with separately.

LUSOTUR
SOCIEDADE FINANCEIRA DE TURISMO, S.A.

Rádio VHF
Channels 62, 20
Call signal - VILAMOURA RADIO

Lat.: 37º 04'. IN
Long.: 8º 07'. 3W

Marina de Vilamoura 8125 Quarteira - Portugal - Tel. (089) 30 29 24 / 7 - Fax. (089) 30 29 28

Northern Europe to Azores

Falmouth to Ponta Delgada 1200 m
Falmouth to Horta 1230 m

Favourable conditions should prevail along most of this route during June and July, when most boats make the passage. If southwest winds persist south of England, and a direct course for the Azores is difficult to lay, it might be better to alter plans and make a detour via the Atlantic coast of Spain or Portugal. On the subsequent leg one should then have the benefit of the Portuguese trades. Unless one has access to reliable weather information, the possibility of meeting contrary winds on the way cannot be discounted, so such a detour should be allowed for and the necessary charts carried on board.

Portugal to Azores

Lisbon to Horta 920 m
Vilamoura to Horta 980 m
Lisbon to Ponta Delgada 780 m
Vilamoura to Ponta Delgada 840 m

Conditions are usually favourable along this route, especially during summer when the prevailing northerly winds, the Portuguese trades, normally provide a fast departure from continental Europe. Northerly winds are rarely carried all the way to the Azores, the point at which these diminish depending on the position of the Azores high. Light winds or calms will be met if the high extends towards Europe, which is more likely at the beginning of summer. Once the ridge of high pressure has been crossed, southwest winds may be encountered closer to the islands.

Mediterranean to Azores

Gibraltar to Ponta Delgada 990 m
Gibraltar to Horta 1120 m

Passing through the notorious Straits of Gibraltar should pose no problem during easterly winds, which are the prevailing winds of summer. Because of the difficulty associated with a westbound passage through the Straits of Gibraltar, boats usually stop in Gibraltar to wait for the right conditions. Steadier conditions can only be expected after Cape St Vincent has been passed and one has reached the Atlantic proper. From there on conditions should be similar to those for the routes from mainland Portugal.

Madeira to Azores

Funchal to Santa Maria 480 m
Funchal to Ponta Delgada 530 m

During the summer months, conditions in the lee of Madeira rarely reflect those at sea, so one should be prepared for variable winds until the western end of the island is reached. From there on one should have the benefit of the prevailing northeasterlies for most of the passage. If southwest winds are forecast at the start, it may be better to wait in Funchal for a change, as such winds usually bring unsettled weather. The small island of Santa Maria is a convenient first landfall if arriving from this direction.

Canaries to Azores

Las Palmas to Ponta Delgada 780 m
Santa Cruz de la Palma to Horta 810 m

The winds of summer will most likely be from the northeast, making this a close hauled passage, especially if leaving from one of the western islands such as La Palma. A contrary current of up to half a knot may also be experienced. A better alternative is to start off from one of the eastern islands, such as Lanzarote, and plan on making a stop in Madeira where one can wait for favourable conditions for the rest of the passage.

Lesser Antilles to Azores

Antigua to Horta 2170 m
St Thomas to Horta 2250 m

An increasing number of boats are making this passage from the Caribbean nonstop rather than following the traditional route via Bermuda. On leaving any of the islands in the Eastern Caribbean, and this includes the Virgins, one should set a northeast course. This should not be too difficult as the trade winds are mostly south of east when this passage is usually made, in May or June. Southeasterly winds may be carried for most of the way, although the likelihood of calms increases as one enters the Horse Latitudes. This is the time when a good reserve of fuel can make up for the lack of wind. Conditions in the vicinity of the Azores are difficult to predict, but are more likely to be southwesterly winds in May or early June, with the frequency of northeasterly winds increasing as summer progresses.

Bermuda to Azores

Bermuda to Horta 1800 m

Because Bermuda is situated to the south of the area of prevailing westerly winds, the recommended strategy is to make as much as northing as possible on leaving Bermuda in the hope of finding favourable winds around latitude 40°N.

The advantage of a northern route is a greater probability of west or southwest winds and a favourable current. The disadvantages are the higher frequency of gale force winds and a colder, and possibly wetter, passage compared to a course which does not go above the latitude of Bermuda. Opinions are divided as to which is the best course to follow and so some skippers take the easier alternative and stick to the rhumb line, which at least has warmer weather, even if the winds rarely ensure a fast passage and one may have to use the engine to get out of calms or light headwinds. If a northern route is chosen, it is advisable not to sail beyond 40°N before the 50°W meridian has been crossed due to the risk of encountering ice in the early part of summer.

USA and Canada to Azores

Newport to Horta 1960 m
Norfolk to Horta 2230 m
St. Johns to Horta 1250 m

The advantage of a direct route from North America to the Azores, as opposed to one which goes via Bermuda, is that the area of prevailing westerlies can be reached sooner, especially by boats leaving from north of the Chesapeake Bay. South of Chesapeake it is debatable whether stopping in Bermuda makes much difference. Depending on weather conditions, the first objective on leaving the east coast, is to reach a theoretical point approximately at 40°N, 60°W as quickly as possible. From there the same directions apply as for the direct route from Bermuda.

Boats leaving from ports south of the Chesapeake Bay usually ride the Gulf Stream for part of the way before reaching that recommended point and turn east once steady westerly winds have been found. During summer, when the Azores high extends farther north, consistent westerlies will only be found in higher latitudes and this should be considered when deciding on the course to take. If making the passage from July onwards, the risk of early hurricanes must be born in mind, especially if leaving from southern ports. From May to July mostly south or southwest winds can be expected for the first part of the passage with lighter, or easterly winds, closer to the Azores. A rhumb line course along a southerly route is only recommended if one is prepared to motor in the calm or light wind conditions bound to be encountered in lower latitudes.

GETTING AWAY

There are three main routes taken by boats leaving the Azores; to Northern Europe, the Mediterranean and North America. Boats bound for the English Channel and beyond usually have the tougher trip as the prevailing winds in summer are from the northeast. The same winds make a passage to the Mediterranean an easier affair. A spell of northeasterly winds would certainly help anyone setting off for America, but such conditions rarely last for long. In July 1993 a prolonged spell of easterly winds made life very hard for the boats trying to reach the Azores from Bermuda, but were highly appreciated by the few boats sailing in the opposite direction. Whatever one's destination, it pays to wait for a favourable long term forecast, especially in summer, as weather conditions can be predicted fairly accurately for up to one week ahead.

Azores to Northern Europe
Horta to Crosshaven 1120 m
Ponta Delgada to Crosshaven 1140 m
Horta to Falmouth 1230 m
Ponta Delgada to Falmouth 1190 m

The prevailing summer winds on leaving the Azores are northeast and therefore most northbound passages are close hauled. Unless one leaves with a long term forecast of southwest winds, a direct course for the English Channel is rarely possible. Nor is such a course advisable, as the westerly winds and east flowing current that prevail in higher latitudes may set the boat into the Bay of Biscay. North of the archipelago calms or light winds are frequent in summer, their extent depending on the position of the Azores high.

The accepted routine on leaving the Azores is to sail due north until steady westerly winds are encountered and not to join the great circle route for the English Channel before latitude 45°N has been crossed. Boats bound for Ireland usually follow the same tactic. If calms or light winds are encountered, one should be prepared to motor and make the desired northing.

Azores to Portugal
Horta to Lisbon 920 m
Horta to Vilamoura 980 m
Ponta Delgada to Lisbon 780 m
Ponta Delgada to Vilamoura 840 m

Favourable conditions may be expected for most of this passage, although on closing with the Portuguese coast, the strong Portuguese trades, which blow throughout the summer, combined with a south setting current, will call for some hard windward work to reach ports north of Cape St Vincent. Reaching the Algarve coast will be somewhat easier, especially as the strength of the northerly winds usually diminishes once Cape St Vincent has been weathered. Occasionally, a southwest breeze blows up on summer afternoons, making it easier to close with the Algarve coast.

Azores to the Mediterranean
Horta to Gibraltar 1120 m
Ponta Delgada to Gibraltar 990 m

Steadier winds can be expected along this route towards the middle of summer, when northeast winds may blow as far as the longitude of Cape St Vincent. At any other time, a spell of southwest winds can be just as likely, which occasionally may be carried as far as the Straits of Gibraltar, but usually peter out as the system generating them passes overhead. If a strong *levanter* (easterly wind) is blowing when approaching Gibraltar, one can seek shelter in one of the ports in the Bay of Cadiz.

Azores to Madeira
Horta to Funchal 680 m
Ponta Delgada to Funchal 530 m
Santa Maria to Funchal 480m

The winds between these two Portuguese outposts are usually favourable and the likelihood of northeast winds increases as one approaches Madeira. A good starting point for the passage to Madeira is the island of Santa Maria.

Azores to Canaries
Horta to Las Palmas 910 m
Ponta Delgada to Arrecife 810 m

Both winds and current are usually favourable on this passage. If planning to cruise the Canaries it is best to sail first to one of the eastern islands, such as Lanzarote, as the northeast winds, which prevail over the islands in summer, will then be mostly to one's advantage while cruising the islands.

Azores to Bermuda
Horta to Bermuda 1800 m

A reliable long term forecast should be obtained before leaving on this passage and if westerly winds are expected it is

Welcome to the BIGGEST little Chandlery in Paradise !!!

COMPREHENSIVE YACHT SERVICE

Boat-In-Transit Prices - Boatside Service - Daily Pick-Up & Delivery
ALWAYS OPEN TO SERVE CRUISERS...NO SIESTA...NO FIESTA
10 LANGUAGES SPOKEN

SERVICE

Top Yachting takes great pride in providing professional service with a dedicated sense of urgency. Our teams of yacht outfitting, repair, and maintenance engineers focus on quality work AND your scheduled cast-off date. Drawn from boating countries around the world, the Top Yachting Team boasts expertise in yacht problem-solving and solution-making. Top Yachting has all the right products at the right prices to enhance your yachting pleasure.

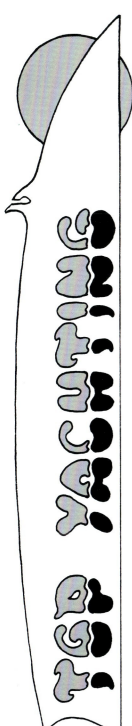

TOP CHANDLERY	TOP ENGINEERING	TOP TRONICS
Whatever you need, the Top Yachting Chandlery Champions will find it for you and get it to you at a fair price, FAST, FAST, FAST. Top Chandlery also serves as the communications centre between you and what and whom you need...from the professionals at Top Engineering and Top Tronics, to the supplier that makes the parts or pieces you want. Top Chandlery are also the specialists in getting your equipment quickly and inexpensively through the "Boat-In-Transit" system...no tax or duty! If Top Channdlery doesn't have it - they'll source it!	The men with the "Golden Hands" can do it all and do it excellently. Top Engineering ostracises osmosis, exorcises electrolysis, synthesises substrates (aluminium, fibreglass, rubber, steel, wood), massages mechanics (compressors, generators, hydraulics, inboards, outboards, pumps, fridges), Picassos paint jobs, revolutionises rigging and are simply magnificent with air-conditioners, watermakers, water filter systems, dinghy repairs, etc., etc., etc. Top Engineering guarantees, "if it can break, we can unbreak it!"	The Top Tronics Team (under the enlightened leadership of The Wizard) are Masters of the Universe of Electrics and Electronics. Their wealth of expertise can help you find the right piece of equipment or repair any make or model. If the mysteries of your electrics and electronics problems have stumped the others, The Wizard and his Trons can source and solve. Don't forget to ask for the Top Tronics free catalogue - the best products and prices in the world! Give them a try...you will be amazed.

Top Yachting acts as their own freight agent, allowing goods to be processed within 24 hours of arrival at the airport. We can get it from the manufacturer to your boat faster and cheaper than anyone else. And remember, Top Yachting buys direct from over 50 manufacturers of quality marine products, avoiding several levels of intermediaries - in other words, you will save money!

Top Yachting welcomes the cruising community to our slice of paradise. Sail, drive, bicycle, or walk to lovely Puerto Mogan and visit our beautiful showroom. We know you will be impressed...and we will be pleased to see you.

We Cater to Cruisers !!!

SEND FOR YOUR SUPER DISCOUNT MAIL ORDER CATALOGUE

TOP YACHTING, S.A. — Tel: Int. 34 (9) 28 - 56 51 46 — Fax: Int. 34 (9) 28 - 56 52 00
Local, 96 - Puerto Mogan — "THE **BIGGEST** LITTLE CHANDLERY IN PARADISE !!!"

better to wait for a change rather than beat one's way westward. Although Horta is a good starting point as it has better provisioning and repair facilities, a convenient alternative is the port of Lajes, on Flores, which has been greatly improved. In summer it is best to wait for a spell of northeast winds, which will ensure a fast start to the passage. Later, if westerly winds are encountered, it is better to stay on the starboard tack rather than make too much northing as this puts one into the area of prevailing westerlies and also the eastsetting Gulf Stream.

Azores to USA and Canada

Horta to Newport 1980 m
Horta to St Johns 1250 m

A difficult decision to make on leaving the Azores is whether or not to stop in Bermuda. If a stop in Bermuda is envisaged, the same suggestions apply as for the above route. Otherwise, it is probably better to go with the weather and sail a course which does not take one too far away from Bermuda, so as to be able to stop there if necessary. A stop in Bermuda is attractive primarily for boats bound for ports south of New York, otherwise the detour makes little sense. Boats bound for Canadian ports have a tough trip ahead and might be better off by closing as quickly as possible with the American coast and then sailing along it to their port of destination.

WEATHER

The Azores have a typical Atlantic climate of which the dominant feature is the area of high pressure or anticyclone named after them. The position of the Azores high varies with the season, being more northerly in summer and more southerly in winter and spring, usually lying to the south or southwest of the islands. During summer the weather is particularly affected by the strength and location of this high. A strong high will push the barometer to 1030 mb or above, which will result in pleasant and warm weather, but little wind for sailing. At other times, when the high is weak, the weather is changeable and wet. Sudden drops in the barometer accompanied by southerly winds foretell the approach of a depression, when the wind will veer from southwest to northwest. Lows pass over the Azores from west to east with winds seldom exceeding 30 knots.

During the early summer the winds are mostly from the southwest becoming predominantly northeasterly in July and August, their strength around 10 knots and frequent calms. By September, the winds are back in the southwest quarter and their strength gradually increases.

The Azores have a pleasant climate, with no extremes of temperature. The average temperatures range from 14° to 22°C, with the coldest month being February and the hottest August. The highest temperatures have been recorded when the Azores anticylone is well established, covers a large area, has a southwest to northeast orientation and is situated to the southwest of the archipelago. Such a situation causes a flow of tropical sea air and light winds from the southwest. On the other hand, the lowest temperatures occur when depressions pass between the Azores and Ireland. In such a situation cold polar air is drawn into the area, the weather is unsettled, wet and cold. Freezing temperatures have never been recorded in living memory, although during the winter night temperatures usually reach single figures.

Sea water temperatures cover a similarly narrow range, with the highest recordings in August and September, when the average hovers around 22°C, while the lowest is in February and March, when the average fluctuates between 15°C and 16°C.

The strongest winds recorded in the Azores occurred on 15 February 1988 when a violent storm hit the island of Faial with gusts of up to 150 knots. Fortunately the storm had a very narrow path and so the damage was mostly limited to the areas directly hit, mainly inland where it left a path of destruction with trees bereft of their crowns as if a giant lawnmower had moved across the island. The gigantic seas generated by the storm reached 20 metres (60 ft) in Porto Pim, on the south coast of Faial.

Occasionally tropical storms originating in the Caribbean reach as far east as the Azores as they move northeast across the Atlantic. The most recent occurred on 26 September 1992 when hurricane Charlie, moving northeast through the archipelago, generated winds of over 50 knots with gusts of 75 knots in a 60 mile wide band which passed between the islands of Terceira and São Miguel. Outside that relatively narrow band, the winds averaged 35 to 40 knots. At its lowest the depression measured 995 millibars.

Although similar in general terms, there are some differences in weather between the individual islands. At Santa Cruz das Flores southerly winds prevail throughout the year, with the second most common winds blowing from the north. In Horta southwesterly winds prevail in all months of the year. In Angra do Heroísmo, on the south coast of Terceira, westerly winds prevail for most of the year, with southwesterly winds predominating in February and between June and September. On the north coast of Terceira, northerly winds prevail for most of the year, except from December to March when the prevailing winds are from the southwest and south. At Ponta Delgada, on the south coast of São Miguel, northeasterly winds prevail between April and November, while southwesterlies predominate in the other months. Finally, in Santa Maria the prevailing winds between May and November are from the northeast, while southerly winds predominate in December and January and westerlies in February and March.

Generally, it can be stated that in the western group (Flores and Corvo) and central group (Faial, Pico, São Jorge, Graciosa and Terceira) the prevailing winds are from the western quarter,

GIBRALTAR'S FRIENDLY CHANDLERY RUN BY EXPERIENCED, KNOWLEDGABLE YACHTSMEN

Electronics • General Chandlery • Repairs & Maintenance • Deliveries
Caretaking • Insurance • Clothing • Slip facilities • Liferaft servicing
ALWAYS WILLING TO HELP

THE YACHTSMAN CHANDLERY

Marina Bay & Queensway Quay, Gibraltar. Tel & Fax (350) 70252 while in the eastern group (São Miguel and Santa Maria) northeasterly winds predominate. The explanation lies in the fact that the first two groups (western and central) usually find themselves on the western side of the Azores anticyclone, while the eastern group lies beneath the eastern side of the same anticyclone. The highest frequency of calms occurs in July, except in Ponta Delgada where it occurs in August, while the lowest frequency of calms throughout the archipelago is in March. The highest average wind speeds have been recorded in Santa Maria and the lowest in Ponta Delgada, but in both cases this is a result not so much of their geographical position, but local factors. Wind speeds in summer rarely exceed 15 knots, while gale force winds occur mostly in winter, with their frequency down to almost nil between June and August.

As one would expect from such high volcanic islands, there are many local land and sea breezes depending on individual features and weather conditions. The high peak of Pico particularly gives the impression that it is constantly generating its own weather. Much of the higher land on the islands is often wreathed in clouds as moisture laden air hits the islands and it is rare to see the complete peak of Pico without some sort of cloud. A strange mushroom shaped cloud covering the peak is said to foretell a change in weather.

The presence of low cloud means that visibility is often reduced and a sea mist can hide the islands, so that Pico may be invisible from Horta, five miles away.

Occasionally visibility is so bad that the airports are closed. This is a point that should be born in mind when making landfall. There is no better description than that by Eric Hiscock of his landfall on São Miguel in *Voyaging Under Sail*.

The day was bright and sunny with a vivid blue sea and sky and a sharp horizon, and I guessed the visibility to be about 40 miles, or more. The island rises to 3,600 feet, and at 0600 it was by account less than 40 miles away, so I naturally expected to sight it soon. But the morning wore on with an empty horizon, and although terns visited us and my wife... could smell pines and sweet-scented flowers, we had no sight of land or of any cloud in the sky to suggest the proximity of land; and not until we has sailed to within 15 miles of it did the island appear faintly through its unsuspected shroud of mist, which was the same colour as the sky.

The weather can change quite quickly and a local folk saying claims that in the Azores there are four seasons in one day. Local observations have noted a marked change for the better in weather conditions. In last three years the weather has been much drier, which also accounts for the water shortage experienced on some of the islands. In the past the seasons were more clearly defined, and the weather was also more settled, whereas now it is much more changeable, but more pleasant.

Looking at all the above factors, one can conclude that the best time to visit the Azores is between the middle of June and end of August. Occasionally July can be windless, so August is probably the best choice, when one can have good sailing winds and both the air and seawater temperatures are highest.

AROUND THE ISLANDS

In spite of the ever increasing number of yachts stopping in the Azores, only a tiny fraction cruise around the islands and usually leave without calling at any other port or island outside of their first landfall, which in most cases is the

marina at Horta. Over one thousand yachts called at Horta in 1993, and more than 90 per cent left without stopping at any other island. A few sailed over to the island of São Miguel and spent a few days in the new marina at Ponta Delgada. The opening of this new marina appears to have only turned the Azores from a one stop to a two stop destination.

A cruise around the islands has its starting point very much dependent on where one is coming from. If arriving from across the Atlantic, as the majority of yachts do, it makes sense to make one's landfall on Flores and visit the two westernmost islands first, as these are 140 miles from the central group. Similarly if arriving from Madeira, the Mediterranean or mainland Portugal, the two easternmost islands of Santa Maria and São Miguel are the logical first stops. As the summer winds are variable, the central group of islands are best cruised taking advantage of the prevailing wind conditions.

There are virtually no offshore dangers and due to the high nature of the islands, there is great depth until within 50 metres of the shore. This means that one can often sail along the coasts and admire the dramatic scenery from close to. Another pleasure of sailing in the Azores is the abundant marine life and it is rare to make any passage between the islands in summer without sighting dolphins or whales. Filling up with water or fuel outside of the two marinas is not easy and this should be born in mind when planning a cruise.

One detraction to the Azores as a cruising destination is their remoteness from both continental Europe and North America. Indeed this can be a problem, especially for those short of time, but with a little planning even this obstacle can be overcome. With two excellent marinas, where the boat could be left in complete safety between seasons, a summer cruise in the Azores could be the start of a longer stay in the islands.

Such a plan should appeal to both European and North American sailors. The latter may also consider spending all summer cruising the Azores and leave the boat for the winter either afloat in Horta or ashore in the new marina in Ponta Delgada. Both marinas are cheaper than any on mainland Europe and much cheaper than any comparative marina in the USA. With weekly flights from Terceira to Boston, one does not even have to fly to Lisbon to catch a transatlantic flight, while there are daily flights via Lisbon to most European destinations. The following spring one is poised to sail either to Northern Europe or the Mediterranean.

A summer cruise in the Azores is highly recommended, not only because weather conditions are ideal, but also because all that is best about the Azores happens in summer; the flowers are in full bloom, the water is warm, whalewatching is at its best, there are plenty of fiestas on every island and

Horta has its unforgettable Sea Week, to name just a few of the attractions that make the Azores a summer destination hard to beat.

PORT FACILITIES

Outside of the two marinas, at Horta and Ponta Delgada, which have been built to the highest standard, facilities are generally rudimentary. Mooring buoys are available only in a few ports and so one should be prepared to anchor and go ashore by dinghy. Coming alongside is permitted in most ports if there is space, but the quays have been built for ships, with large tyre fenders and few points of access to the high quay above. If wishing to stay alongside a quay, permission must be sought from the local Capitania.

There are three port authorities (Juntas), which are financially autonomous organisations under the tutelage of the Regional Government, directly under the Secretariat of Public Works. The Juntas, based in Horta (JAPH), Angra do Heroísmo (JAPAH) and Ponta Delgada (JAPD) are responsible for the following ports:-

JAPH: São Jorge: Velas and Calheta; Pico: Madalena and São Roque; Faial: Horta; Flores: Santa Cruz and Lajes; Corvo: Vila Nova.

JAPAH: Terceira: Angra do Heroísmo and Praia da Vitória; Graciosa: Praia.

JAPD: São Miguel: Ponta Delgada; Santa Maria: Vila do Porto.

The mooring buoys laid down in these ports by the Juntas are usually red or orange and often can be identified by the initials of the authority i.e. JAPH.

The marina at Horta is administered by the Port Authority (JAPH), whereas the new marina in Ponta Delgada has been franchised to a private company. There are moves to franchise Horta Marina as well, although this is being lobbied against. Also there are calls for a marina to be built in Angra do Heroísmo. All other ports are administered by the Secretariat for Agriculture and Fisheries.

Fuel and Water

Facilities for yachts in most ports are virtually nonexistent with neither fuel nor water outlets on the quays, so one has to be self-sufficient in every respect. This should be born in mind when leaving one of the two marinas and one should leave with full tanks of both fuel and water. These items are available in all ports, but they have to be carried in jerrycans. The fuel stations are often some distance from the port, although most ports have at least one water tap, normally on the ramp where the fishing boats are hauled out.

Repair Facilities

Repair facilities are concentrated in the large ports, with the best being in Horta, Ponta Delgada and Angra do Heroísmo, and, to some extent, at Madalena, on Pico, due to the presence of a large offshore fishing fleet. Nautical equipment and spares are not easily available, so all essential spares should be carried on board. There are no hoists in the Azores and any hauling out has to be done by crane in one of the larger ports. It is therefore advisable not to plan on hauling out for routine maintenance work.

Costs

Because of the lack of facilities for yachts, there is no provision for port charges, either for the use of mooring buoys or for coming alongside the quay. The exception are the two marinas, at Ponta Delgada and Horta, where docking fees are approximately half of the equivalent European marina and one third of US marinas. There are no charges for clearing in or out, nor overtime charges by customs or immigration officials. The only charge is the initial 120 escudos (50 pence or 75 US cents) for the transit log, so if one does not go into one of the marinas, which admittedly is quite unlikely, the cruising costs will be close to nil. For anyone sailing on a limited budget, this is undoubtedly cruising at its best!

GENERAL INFORMATION

BUOYAGE IALA A

LOCAL TIME GMT - 1. April to September summer time, GMT.

CURRENCY Portuguese escudo of 100 centavo, written 00$00. The exchange rate in October 1993 was £1 = 250$00 and 1US$ = 170$00.

ELECTRICITY 220V, 50 cycles

BUSINESS HOURS
Banks: 0830-1500 Monday to Friday
Shops: 0900-1230, 1400-1800 Monday to Friday, Saturday morning
Government offices: 0900-1230, 1400-1730 Monday to Friday

PUBLIC HOLIDAYS

1 January: New Year's Day
Good Friday
25 April: National Day
1 May: Labour Day
Corpus Christi
Whit Monday - Autonomy Day
10 June: Portugal Day
15 August: Assumption
5 October: Republic Day
1 November: All Saints Day
1 December: Independence Day
8 December: Immaculate Conception
25 December: Christmas Day
There are also various municipal holidays on each island.

COMMUNICATIONS

To dial the Azores from abroad dial IDD code 351 (Portugal) followed by the area code for the island:
92 Faial, Pico, Flores, Corvo;
95 Terceira, Graciosa, São Jorge;
96 São Miguel, Santa Maria.

International calls can be made from post offices, hotels and some metered public phones in cafés, marinas and yacht clubs. The metered calls at the post offices are the cheapest rate for telephoning. International calls can also be made with phonecards from public telephones, which are found in most places. It is necessary to dial 00 for an international line, followed by the country code and area code. For assistance or information dial 098 (Intercontinental) or 099 (Europe).

Stamps can be bought from post offices or where a green *correio* sign is shown. Faxes can be received or sent from post offices in the major towns.

TRANSPORT

Public transport is excellent on the larger islands (São Miguel, Terceira and Faial) and the local bus service provides the cheapest way of exploring the islands. Bus timetables are available from the tourist information offices and services are remarkably punctual.

Taxis, easily identified as black with green roofs, are plentiful and reasonably priced. If using a taxi for a longer trip such as a round island tour, it is advisable to agree on the price beforehand.

The central group of islands are linked by ferries. The Horta to Madalena ferry runs several times a day and is often used by sailors to visit the island of Pico, while leaving their boat in Horta Marina.

Car Hire

Car hire companies are found throughout the islands except on Corvo and renting a car may be the best way to see the interior of the islands. Prices vary and start from 2,800 to 4,000 escudos a day for the smallest type of car. Mileage is 25-40 escudos per kilometre for a small car. The driver must be over 23 or 25 years old, depending on the company concerned, and should have held a valid driving licence for at least a year. The car hire companies are mainly small local companies and not all of them accept payment by credit card. Those that do not may ask for a cash deposit.

Collision Damage Waiver (CDW) can be taken in most cases, but usually this does not cover the hirer for the excess, which amounts to between 250,000 and 500,000 escudos. The hirer is responsible for this amount unless liability is accepted by the other party in an accident, which may be difficult to achieve. With little traffic outside of towns and slow speeds, it is worth considering saving one's money and not take out this additional insurance as even if one does, one is still responsible for paying for all minor damage, such as broken mirrors, windows, missing hubcaps or scratches. This does mean that one should be extremely careful when taking over a car and make sure that any damage or scratches are noted down on the contract.

Flights

The national Portuguese airline TAP has daily flights from Lisbon to São Miguel, Faial and Terceira. International flights into Lisbon usually connect with one of these flights, so one can normally reach any of the islands on the same day. There are also direct flights to Boston from Terceira, especially in the summer months. The local airline SATA operates within the Azores and there are frequent flights between all islands.

Flight Information

Santa Maria	82497
São Miguel	23261
Terceira	52011, 53013
Graciosa	72458
São Jorge	42395
Pico	622413
Faial	93112
Flores	52151

Walks

The unspoilt countryside, beautiful scenery and pleasant climate make the Azores a walker's paradise. There are suggested walks for every island and a couple of books describing these. However, signs are not very prolific and in many places are missing. As paths may have been ploughed up or have overgrown beyond recognition, it would certainly help taking a handheld compass along, although having one's portable GPS as well might be a bit of an exaggeration. Walking shoes are, of course, highly recommended.

MEDICAL

Emergency medical treatment is free. EC nationals will not be charged for a hospital bed, but non-EC nationals may have to pay.

For non-emergency treatment and consultations, a fee is charged.

Emergency numbers

Emergencies 115
Medical Centres/Pharmacies 118
Police:

Santa Maria	8 21 22
São Miguel	2 20 22
Terceira	2 20 22
Graciosa	7 21 09
São Jorge	4 23 39
Pico (Madalena)	9 22 05
Pico (São Roque)	6 41 15
Faial	2 20 22
Flores	5 21 15

BANKING

The Banco Comercial dos Açores is the largest bank in the Azores and has branches in all main towns. Travellers cheques and cash can be changed at all banks, most of which also have cash dispensers outside which will dispense cash using a cashpoint card. Credit cards are accepted in many places such as the bigger supermarkets, restaurants and car hire firms, but one should check first, as some do not accept credit cards.

DIPLOMATIC MISSIONS

Ponta Delgada:
Austria: 12 Rua Carvalho Araújo, Tel. 27687
Belgium: Rua de Santana, Lote 6, Tel. 24846
Brazil: 5-1 Av. Infante Dom Henrique, Tel. 23321
Canada: Av. Infante Dom Henrique, Tel. 24030

BANCO COMERCIAL DOS AÇORES

Electronic money transfers, SWIFT, fixed-term and instant deposits, investments. Take advantage of our offshore banking. Your full service bank in the Azores.

	BRANCH	ADDRESS	POST CODE	TELEPHONE	FAX
AZORES					
SANTA MARIA	Vila Do Porto	R. Dr. Luis Bettencourt, 37	9580 VILA DO PORTO	096-82406/82430	096-82265
	Posto de Câmbios	Aeroporto de Sta Maria	9580 VILA DO PORTO	096-82777	096-82265
SÃO MIGUEL	Matriz	Largo da Matriz, 42-43	9500 PONTA DELGADA	096-629070	096-629799
	Largo 2 Março	R. Diário dos Açores, 24	9500 PONTA DELGADA	096-629466/456	096-629136
	Calheta	R. Eng. José Cordeiro, 83-87A	9500 PONTA DELGADA	096-35441/6	096-35448
	Lagoa	Av. Infante D. Henrique, 48B	9560 LAGOA	096-92870/77	096-92125
	Vila Franca do Campo	Largo Bento de Gois, 14	9680 FRANCA DO CAMPO	096-53103/52578	096-52633
	Ribeira Grande	R. El Rei D. Carlos I, 46-56	9600 RIBEIRA GRANDE	096-472540/640	096-473595
	Nordeste	R. António Alves Oliveira, 30-32	9630 NORDESTE	096-488510/11	096-488512
	Povoação	Largo do Jardim Municipal	9650 POVOAÇÃO	096-55351/4	096-55355
	Furnas	Largo do Teatro, 4	9675 FURNAS	096-54171	096-54171
	Ribeira Quente	R. Além Ribeira, 1	9675 FURNAS	096-54296	096-55355
TERCEIRA	Angra do Heroísmo	R. da República, 32-34	9700 ANGRA DO HEROÍSMO	095-27035/9	095-22701
	Praia da Vitória	R. De Jesus, 13-15	9760 PRAIA DA VITÓRIA	095-53178/53192	095-53805
	Lajes (Terceira)	Terminal Militar Base Aérea, 4	9760 PRAIA DA VITÓRIA	095-52136/53315	095-52733
GRACIOSA	Santa Cruz (Graciosa)	R. Cons Jacinto Cândido, 24	9880 STA CRUZ DA GRACIOSA	095-72305/72372	095-72488
SÃO JORGE	Velas	R. Dr. Manuel Arriaga, 22	9800 VELAS	095-42369/42206	095-42200
	Calheta	R. Manuel Augusto da Cunha	9850 CALHETA	095-46415/46540	095-46248
PICO	Madalena	Largo Jaime Ferreira	9950 MADALENA	092-622389/390	092-622896
	Lajes do Pico	Largo General Lacerda Machado	9930 LAJES DO PICO	092-672169/672363	092-672116
	Piedade	Curral da Pedra	9930 LAJES DO PICO	092-666280	092-666489
	S. Roque do Pico	Rua do Cais	9940 S. ROQUE DO PICO	092-642171/2	092-642444
FAIAL	Horta	R. Com. Ernesto Rebeldo, 4	9900 HORTA	092-22011/3	092-23681
FLORES	Santa Cruz (Flores)	R. Senador André de Freitas, 4	9970 STA CRUZ DAS FLORES	092-52355/52174	092-52674
	Lajes das Flores	R. Dr. José Freitas Pimentel	9960 LAJES FLORES	092-53238/40	092-53274
CORVO	Vila Nova	Largo da Cancela	9980 CORVO	092-56129	092-56129
PORTUGAL					
LISBOA	Miguel Bombarda	Av. Miguel Bombarda, 123A	1000 LISBOA	01-3158205/7	01-3158210
	Lapa	R. dos Navegantes, 19	1200 LISBOA	01-3968081/2	01-3977778
PORTO	Porto	R. Formosa, 409-417	4000 PORTO	02-2086825/32	02-2086824
USA					
FALL RIVER	Fall River	1531 Pleasant Street	02723 FALL RIVER, MASS. USA	001-5086735881	001-5086784766
BERMUDA					
HAMILTON	Hamilton	19 Queen St / Somers Mort. & Fin.	UM11 HAMILTON, BERMUDA	001-8092921841	001-8092926950

Branches in every island, also in Lisbon, Oporto, Bermuda and Fall River (USA).

General Information

Denmark: 8-1 Praceta Gonçalo Velho, Tel. 24291
Finland: Rua António Borges, Tel. 23365
France: 57 Coronel Miranda, Tel. 24896
Germany: 18 Travessa do Desterro, Tel. 23935
Italy: 35 Rua Luis Soares de Sousa, Tel. 24558
Netherlands: 13 Largo Vasco Bensaúde, Tel. 22201
Norway: 61 Largo da Matriz, Tel. 23321
Spain: Rua Direita, Fajã de Baixo, Tel. 32640
Sweden: Rua Senhora da Rosa, Fajã de Baixo, Tel. 31301
Turkey: 75 Rua Dr. Aristides da Mota, Tel. 22667
United Kingdom: Largo Vasco Bensaúde, Tel. 22201
United States: Av. Infante Dom Henrique, Tel. 22216

Horta:
France: 1 Travessa São Francisco, Tel. 22926
Italy: Rua Consul Dabney, Tel 22770

Autohelm
Your Canarian Sales/Service Representative
★★★★★
AMAZING "BOAT-IN-TRANSIT" PRICES!
★★★★★
Ask for "The Wizard"
★★★★★
We Cater To Cruisers!
SEE PAGE 15

TOP YACHTING, S.A. "THE **BIGGEST** LITTLE CHANDLERY IN PARADISE!!!"
Local 96 - Puerto Mogan - Tel: Int. 34 (9) 28 - 56 51 46 - Fax: Int. 34 (9) 28 - 56 52 00

VHF RADIO STATIONS

NAME OF STATION	INDICATIVE	LISTENING CHANNEL	WORKING CHANNEL
VILA DO PORTO (Capitania)	Postrad VIPORTO	16	11
PONTA DELGADA	Postrad DELGADA	16	11
PONTA DELGADA (Pilots)	Pilotos PONTA DELGADA	16	14
PICO DA BARROSA (Radio)	São Miguel RADIO	16	25, 26, 27
ANGRA DO HEROISMO (Capitania)	Postrad ANGRA	16	11
SANTA CRUZ DE GRACIOSA (Capitania)	Postrad GRACIOSA	16	11
VELAS (Capitania)	Postrad VELAS	16	11
HORTA (Radionaval)	Radnaval HORTA	16	11
HORTA (Pilots)	Pilotos HORTA	14	14
FAIAL (Radio)	Faial RÁDIO	16	23,25,26,28
PICO (Radio)	Pico RÁDIO	16	24,25,26,27
LAJES DO PICO (Capitania)	Postrad LAJES	16	11
SÃO ROQUE DE PICO (Capitania)	Postrad ROQUE	16	11
MADALENA (Posto Maritimo)	Postrad MADALENA	16	11
FLORES (Radionaval)	Radnaval FLORES	16	11
SANTA CRUZ DAS FLORES (Capitania)	Postrad FLORES	16	11
CORVO (Radio)	Postrad CORVO	16	11

ENTRY PROCEDURE

PORTS OF ENTRY
Santa Maria
Vila do Porto   36°56'N 25°09'W
São Miguel
Ponta Delgada   37°44'N 25°40'W
Terceira
Angra do Heroísmo 38°39'N 27°13'W
Praia da Vitória   38°44'N 27°03'W
São Jorge Velas   38°40'N 28°12'W
Graciosa Praia   39°03'N 27°58'W
Faial Horta   38°32'N 28°38'W
Flores Santa Cruz 39°27'N 31°07'W

PROCEDURE ON ARRIVAL

The Q flag should be flown at the first port of entry into the Azores, unless coming from Portugal or Madeira. Yachts must clear in at one of the ports of entry where a transit log will be issued. In all ports of call in the Azores visited subsequently, the transit log must be taken along and presented to the local Guarda Fiscal office. In larger ports, the Capitania should also be visited, and sometimes the Policia Maritima.

The Guarda Fiscal, which is responsible for both customs and immigration, is being reorganised and may change its name to that of Brigada Fiscal.

The Capitania or Delegação Maritima is a military body which administers the waters and coasts as well as harbours and ports.

The Junta (Port Authority) is a civil administration in charge of installations and buildings in the ports.

Horta Marina: On arrival yachts should berth alongside the reception quay (minimum depth 3 metres). The marina office is open 0800-1200, 1300-2000 (every day in the high season April to June). The offices of the Capitania and Guarda Fiscal are next to the marina office on the same quay, open 0800-1230, 1400-2000. The marina office should be visited first to receive instructions where to berth once clearance is completed. Yachts arriving after office hours should wait at the reception quay until the next morning.

On departure, one should first pay the marina fees, then take the receipt to the Guarda Fiscal and the Capitania.

Ponta Delgada Marina: On arrival yachts should berth alongside the reception dock, where both the Guarda Fiscal and Capitania have offices. During marina office hours, 0800-1800 daily, the marina office should be contacted first to be allocated a berth. Outside of office hours, a Guarda Fiscal officer is on 24 hour duty and will clear boats in at any time, for which there is no charge.

In all other ports the Guardia Fiscal and Capitania offices are close to the port and should be visited as soon as possible after arrival. It is not normally necessary to come alongside for clearance.

CUSTOMS

Firearms must be declared.

There are no restrictions on animals being allowed ashore, but a rabies innoculation certificate is required.

Yachts may stay for a 6 month period before becoming liable for duty.

The importation of duty free spares for yachts in transit is an aspect which is not as simple as one would expect in a member state of the European Community. Although, in principle, spares imported by a yacht in transit, should be free of duty, this is rarely the case. The main difficulty is that all goods enter the country at Lisbon airport, where customs normally applies duty before the consignment is allowed to continue to the Azores. Usually consignments are delayed for several days at Lisbon aiport and this happens whether they are airfreighted direct or sent via an international courier company.

IMMIGRATION

All visitors should be in possession of a valid passport except for nationals of EC countries who may use their identity cards. Visas are not required for citizens of Western European countries, Argentina, Australia, Brasil, Canada, Chile, Costa Rica, Ecuador, Hungary, Japan, Mexico, New Zealand, Uruguay and the USA. Other nationalities may need to obtain a visa in advance. The visa requirements are more relaxed for persons travelling on a yacht and a visa valid for a limited period may be granted on arrival. Nationals who require a visa and arrive without one should attempt to clear in at one of the major ports of entry, preferably Horta. This concession only applies to those leaving the Azores by yacht and Portuguese visa regulations are adhered to more strictly if crew leave by plane and fly via Lisbon.

CRUISING PERMIT

A transit log, Livrete de Transito, is issued by the Capitania on arrival. There is a charge of 120 escudos for this log, but this is the only charge payable when clearing in or out. All subsequent movements of the yacht are recorded in this log until departure. Yachts must clear in and out of all ports, including harbours on the same island.

Although the Azores, as part of Portugal, are a fully integrated part of the European Community, formalities are still encumbered by a high degree of bureaucracy and yachts are expected to clear in and out of every port. This means a visit on arrival to the local Guarda Fiscal office to show one's transit log and have a form filled in with all the boat details. On departure one only has to inform the Guarda Fiscal of one's intended destination. To save time, anyone intending to stop in more places would be well advised to make a number of photocopies of the form (completed in Portuguese) and then hand it out at every port of arrival.

Restrictions also apply to movement within the archipelago, so one should make sure the Guarda Fiscal is kept informed of one's itinerary. This applies especially if one intends to stop in small ports and anchorages which do not have a Guarda Fiscal office, so before leaving a certain port one should inform the Guarda Fiscal where one intends to stop before arriving at the next bigger port.

The reason why the authorities keep such a tight control on the movement of yachts is the fear of having drugs smuggled in, either from North Africa or the Caribbean. As the Azores are generally drug free, these feelings are understandable but it also means that visiting yachts are submitted to a lot of time consuming bureaucracy. The only redeeming feature is that the officers are invariably polite and helpful, even to the point of waiting on the dockside when one comes in and being there to take one's lines.

DIVING REGULATIONS

Various restrictions apply to diving, while spearfishing is not a welcome sport in most places. Every year there are problems with visitors, on boats or otherwise, who infringe regulations. One must therefore contact the Capitania first and ask for a permit to dive and/or spearfish and at the same time enquire about any restrictions. Spearfishing within 50 metres of a public beach, in ports or in protected areas is prohibited as is spearfishing anywhere with scuba tanks. Only two lobsters per diver may be taken and only within the allowed season and above certain sizes. Diving with air tanks in ports is not permitted. Scuba diving is only allowed if one holds an international certificate. Most yacht clubs have diving sections and it is therefore recommended to dive with one of these clubs or try and find out from their members which restrictions apply locally. Some yacht clubs have compressors for filling tanks and may also rent out equipment.

SANTA MARIA

Santa Maria is the most southern and eastern of the Azorean islands, closest to the mainland of Europe, so it is no surprise that it was the first island to be settled by the Portuguese very soon after being discovered by Diogo de Silves in 1427. Still today it is a good introduction to the Azores. It is the first island in this guide because 1993 is a special year for Santa Maria, being the Quincentenary of the landfall of Christopher Columbus on his successful return from the New World. By the time Columbus arrived in 1493, there were villages scattered all over the island, while the main settlement Vila do Porto had already been given the first town charter in the Azores.

The island's history has been mainly uneventful for the small farming communities, whose only worry was to defend their villages, crops and livestock from various pirates who attacked the island from time to time. In fact Columbus and his men were suspected of being pirates themselves when they sought refuge in the bay of Anjos in February 1493.

In spite of the fortifications built on the island, French, Turkish and Moorish pirates regularly burned, pillaged and carried off prisoners throughout the 16th and 17th centuries. In these early centuries the prosperity of the island was based on the growing of woad, a blue dye exported to Flanders, England and Spain.

The biggest change occurred in Santa Maria relatively recently with the construction of a large airport in 1944. The flat western plateau was taken over by US forces, who built three runways, plus many support buildings such as clubs, a hotel, sports facilities and the semicylindrical Nissen huts of corrugated iron associated with that era, still providing leaky accommodation for airport personnel today. Fortunately building was restricted to the area immediately surrounding the airport, leaving the rest of the island untouched and unspoilt. After the Second World War, this complex was handed over to the islanders and until the building of airports on other islands, for many years Santa Maria was the gateway to the Azores. It is still used by any planes requiring refuelling on the Atlantic run and is also equipped to handle Concorde when necessary, although its importance has declined recently with the longer range of modern jets.

The airport employs 400 of the island's 5000 population and so is an important economic factor. The rest of the population are mainly involved in agriculture or fishing.

Undoubtedly the best time to visit the island is during the Fiesta of Santa Maria, which starts the weekend before 15 August and continues for one week, with a car rally, music festival and yacht race from Ponta Delgada the following weekend. It culminates with a wine harvesting feast in São Lourenço, while the last weekend in August brings everyone together in Maia for the Feast of the Emigrant.

Although the island is one of the smallest in the Azores, only 10 miles long and 5 miles wide, the landscape varies quite considerably. The west and north of the island is drier with many cactus like plants. As one drives up towards the highest point, Pico Alto, the vegetation changes abruptly to thick woods of pine and eucalyptus with luxuriant ferns in the undergrowth. A mist often shrouds these higher slopes, which was a contributing factor to the tragic disaster in 1989 when a Boeing 707 plunged into the hillside when coming in to refuel.

The rest of the island is noticeably

greener and tiny fields surrounded by stone walls are terraced up and down the hillsides, where vegetables, grains, bananas and vines are grown.

In some parts the fields and vines are neglected, due to the migration of a large number of islanders to the USA and Canada. In contrast are the many new houses built in the seaside villages by those settled abroad who return home every summer. Outside of the summer season these villages strung along the beach are almost deserted as many Santa Marians keep two homes, one in the capital Vila do Porto and one on the beach for the summer. The most popular summer retreat is São Lourenço, where terraces of vines come down almost to the sandy beach.

There is a geometric sense to the island from its fields to its houses. Most houses are washed white with a border of pink, blue or more popularly green, picked out around windows, doors and the edges of the house. Sash windows with tiny panes keep with the traditional design, as do the round chimneys.

NAVIGATION

When Columbus anchored in Anjos bay on the north coast, he picked the worst anchorage on the island, witnessed by the fact that he lost two anchors there. Today modern yachts tuck into the new harbour below the main town Vila do Porto on the south coast. Nearby and also protected from northerly winds is an anchorage off the lovely beach at Praia Formosa. Because of a number of offlying rocks, few yachts ever attempt to explore the east coast of Santa Maria, which is a pity as it is undoubtedly the most attractive part of the island. As for the dangers, they are well charted and navigation along this coast presents few problems in settled weather, or with winds blowing from the southwest or west. Under these conditions it is possible to anchor off the charming resort of São Lourenço.

Spectacular scenery continues south

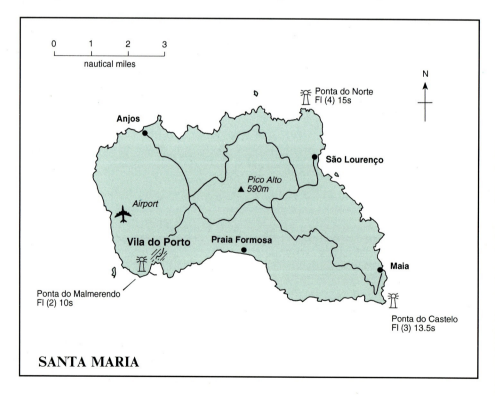

SANTA MARIA

SANTA MARIA AZORES

THE LOGICAL GATEWAY INTO THE AZORES

500 years of welcoming transatlantic sailors

**CÂMARA MUNICIPAL
DE VILA DO PORTO**
9580 VILA DO PORTO
SANTA MARIA – AZORES
TEL (096) 82542 – FAX (096) 82128

Vila do Porto

of São Lourenço, with deep water right up to the base of towering cliffs. A particularly attractive corner is at the foot of Ponta do Espigão, an excellent spot for diving among the offlying rocks. In good weather it is possible to anchor at Porto da Maia and going south from Maia, a beautiful bay surrounded by high cliffs opens up right under the lighthouse on Ponta do Castelo, which is perched on top of the steep headland almost floating among the clouds.

LIGHTS
Vila do Porto Breakwater   36°56'.4N 25°09'.0W   Fl W 5s 15m 5M
Malmerendo   36°56'.4N 25°09'.4W Fl(2) W 10s 50m 10M
Baia dos Anjos   37°00'.2N 25°09'.5W Fl W 3s 13m 10M
Ponta do Norte   37°00'.7N 25°03'.6W Fl(4) W 15s 139m 10M
Baia de São Lourenço   36°59'.5N 25°03'.4W   Fl R 5s 26m 6M
Espigão   36°58'.9N 25°02'.9W Fl W 7s 207m 12M
Gonçalo Velho   36°55'.7N 25°01'.0W Fl(3) W 13.5s 114m 25M

VILA DO PORTO
A massive breakwater, which had to be rebuilt after being destroyed by a violent storm soon after it was first completed, now provides good protection from every direction except the southeast. Overlooking the harbour is a 16th century fort with half a dozen cannons, which used to guard the bay from piratical attack. From the fort the town of Vila do Porto winds up the hill for a mile either side of the main street like a long ribbon, the pavements decorated with black and white mosaics of fish, whales or caravels. The houses lining the street are old, some dating from the 15th century and rendered white, contrasting with the roman style red tiles on the roofs. There are several ornate baroque buildings in the centre around a small square with a bandstand overlooked by the Town Hall which itself occupies a splendid former monastery.

Formalities
The Guarda Fiscal and Capitania offices are both in the building with

green doors on the old quay. Both offices must be visited as soon as possible after arrival whether one comes from another Azorean island or from abroad. If arriving from abroad the transit log can be obtained at the Capitania. If arriving from Madeira or mainland Portugal and already in possession of a transit log, a new one does not have to be issued for the Azores, but the existing one will still need to be stamped.

Port Facilities

Although in theory visiting boats may come alongside the main quay, it is often occupied by a tanker or some other ship, so yachts usually end up at anchor. There are two good spots for anchoring, one in the western part of the harbour, where there are also a number of local moorings, the other one close to the old quay. The latter is more convenient as it is closer to the offices one has to visit on arrival. The best spot for anchoring is between the old quay and the large rocks to the east. Although the port itself is open to southeast, the rocks mentioned above offer some protection from that direction. There are various places where one can land from a dinghy. There are two sets of steps, both very slippery with seaweed, on the older, western quay, and also one set of steps in the new quay by the ramp.

A water tap and outside showers can be found on the ramp. Vila do Porto is a steep kilometre uphill, but the Guarda Fiscal officer will call a taxi if asked.

Yacht Club

The local yacht club has plans to build a club house near the existing ramp and its president is confident that this will happen before the planned World Gamefishing Tournament, which will take place in the waters off Santa Maria in the spring of 1996. There is a slight possibility that the port will have a small marina by then, with its own fuel station and other facilities. In the meantime the yacht club members are more than willing to help visiting sailors and should be contacted if one needs any kind of technical help. The club will also hold incoming mail and, in spite of the absence of a proper club house, will provide the usual services. This includes rental of diving equipment as well as the filling of diving tanks. Clube Naval de Santa Maria, Apartado 40, Vila do Porto. The president, Jorge Botelho, can be contached on Tel. 82166.

Marine Services

Chandlery

Nautisport, Rua Dr João Deus Vieira 35, open Monday to Saturday 1000-1245, 1500-1900, Saturday 1100-1300, stocks some yachting equipment but mostly fishing and diving gear.

Rodrigues & Ricardo, Dr Luis Bettencourt 49, Tel. 82671. A well stocked hardware store with a few chandlery items.

Charts

Nautisport, see above, has a small selection of Portuguese charts.

Diesel Engines

Auto Botelho, Bairro Novo da Lomba, Tel. 82166. The company belongs to the president of the yacht club, an extremely helpful sailor, who should be contacted if help is needed in an emergency.

Remaçor, Rua Dr Manuel Amuda, Tel. 82740.

Outboard Engines

Nautisport, see above, agent for Suzuki.

Elmiro Cunha, Rua Salvaterra, Tel. 82384. Agent for Yamaha.

Auto Botelho, see above, for other makes.

Electrical Repair

Auto Botelho, see above.

Remaçor, see above.

Electronic Repair

Luis Carreiro, Tel. 84322.

Refrigeration Repair

H. Siabra, Cais Vila do Porto. He can be contacted at the refrigeration plant in the port.

Fibreglass Repair

Armando Pacheco, Tel. 86283.

Antonio Lima Martins, Tel. 86291.
Carpentry
Antonio Lopes, a skilled shipwright, can be contacted through the yacht club.
Metalwork
Auto Botelho, see above.
Transmission repair
Auto Botelho, see above.
Fuel
There is no fuel outlet in the port, but Shell, who have a station in town near the park, will deliver larger quantities by tanker to the main quay. Smaller quantities have to be carried in jerrycans. Shell, Tel. 86152.
Gas Filling
Auto Joidil, Rua Nova de Lomba, Tel. 82494.
Globo, Rua Dr Luis Bettencourt 87-93, Tel. 82112. Standard Portuguese bottles and also Camping Gaz.
Diving
Rental of diving equipment and filling of diving tanks: Clube Naval de Santa Maria. Contact the president, Jorge Botelho, Tel. 82166.

Shore Facilities

Provisioning
Supermercado J.C. Baptista, Rua Dr Luis Bettencourt 65-69, open Monday to Friday 0900-1300, 1430-1830, Saturday 0900-1300.
Supermercado T.S. Doubreira, Rua Frei Gonçalo Velho.
Municipal Market, Cotovelho, open Monday to Friday, 0800-1800, Saturday 0800-1300.
Casa Zenite, Rua Dr Luis Bettencourt 60. A greengrocer in the main street.
The bakery is at Rua Dr Luis Bettencourt 11, open Monday to Saturday 0700-1300.
Communications
The main post office is on Rua Teófilo Braga, open Monday to Friday 0900-1230, 1400-1800. Metered telephone calls can be made from here and faxes sent and received (Fax 82590).

Medical
Hospital, Rua João Vieira, Vila do Porto Tel. 82321.
Car Hire
Mariense, Aeroporto, 9580 Vila do Porto, Tel. 82880.
Tourist Information
The Municipal Council has a small information office in Fort São Bras, which overlooks the port.
Laundry
In the absence of a laundry, any of the hotels in Vila do Porto, such as Hotel de Aeroporto or Residencial Santa Maria, will accept laundry at the rates charged to their own clients.
Restaurants
Restaurante Atlantida, Rua Teófilo Braga, Tel. 82330, for local specialities.
Pipas Bar, Rua Dr Luis Bettencourt 25, Tel. 82117, best for grills.

ANJOS
The small village of Anjos is a cluster of whitewashed houses spread around the bay, little different from when the *Niña* dropped anchor there 500 years ago. Set back from the beach is the small chapel of Nossa Senhora dos Anjos, where Columbus and his sailors gave thanks for their delivery from a particularly violent storm and their safe arrival back in the known world. Believed to be the first church built in the Azores and although heavily restored for the Columbus quatercentenary in 1893, the red stone arch at the rear is part of the original church. Above the altar, the original madonna set in a Flemish

Anjos

triptych has been restored for the Quincentenary. A Columbus statue, erected in 1993 opposite the chapel, marks the 500th anniversary of his visit to Anjos. The Admiral's expression and posture, slightly leaning forward with his hand on his heart, has led to a local joke, that he is saying: "Are you *really* sure I've been here before?"

The small quay and ramp hardly deserves the title of a port. There is no depth to come to the quay and, because of the exposed position of the bay, there is always some swell. There is a water tap at the top of the ramp, a small café and shop on the waterfront.

SÃO LOURENÇO

Reputed to be the most attractive resort in the Azores, São Lourenço has the atmosphere of a small fishing village. The village nestles at the foot of a partly collapsed volcanic crater, the high cliffs behind the beach forming a perfect amphitheatre of terraced vineyards.

There is a small port in the northern part of the bay protected by a short breakwater. There is a rock to the southeast of it and an area of shallows over which the seas break. One can anchor immediately in front of the village, or close to the port where one can leave the dinghy at the quay, which has a set of steps. The bay is a very quiet spot, with flat waters when the winds are from the southwest quarter. For most of the year, the place is almost deserted and only comes to life in summer, when holiday makers come over from

São Lourenço

Porto da Maia

neighbouring São Miguel. Many of the houses are owned by people from Vila do Porto, who keep a summer residence in São Lourenço, all of 20 km away.

O Ilheu is a small restaurant serving excellent fish dishes, which the owner, Luis Arruda, serves with chilled white wine served under pressure which imparts it a pleasant fizz.

PORTO DA MAIA

A small port in the north part of the bay north of Maia offers reasonable protection from winds from south through west to north. A short breakwater offers additional protection from the east. There is a small quay and ramp but the entrance is so narrow it is only suitable for local fishing boats. One can anchor close to the breakwater or in the next bay to the north, which is similarly protected in west winds.

Most houses in the village spread along the beach are only occupied in summer. There is a small grocery and a very good restaurant, O Grota, run by Aida Moreira, who returned to her native island after spending several years in the state of New York.

PRAIA FORMOSA

This wide bay on the south coast offers good protection in northerly winds. Believed by many to be the most beautiful beach in the Azores, its yellow sand, clear waters and gradually shelving bottom can certainly compete with some of the best beaches in the Caribbean. An expanding resort has sprung up nearby and there are anchoring depths anywhere in the bay.

SÃO MIGUEL

São Miguel is the largest of the Azorean islands and its capital Ponta Delgada both the busiest harbour and largest town. After Horta it is the next popular port of call for yachts, especially for those arriving from Europe. Although over half of the population of the Azores live on this island, there are still large areas of great natural beauty. The island is lozenge shaped, 65 km long and never more than 16 km wide with two high volcanic areas separated by a lower central area, which is the agricultural heartland of the island with both livestock grazing and crops grown in tidy fields. It is from the green fields in this area that the island derived its local name, *Ilha Verde*, Green Island.

Ponta Delgada was not always the most prominent town, as after the settlement of the island in 1444, the capital was first established at Vila Franca do Campo. Vila Franca thrived until 1522 when an earthquake and mudslide completely destroyed the town, killing the majority of its 5,000 inhabitants. After this disaster, the capital was moved to Ponta Delgada. Vila Franca do Campo recovered and figures prominently in the history of the island, mainly in battles with the Spanish.

In 1582 the Spanish defeated a combined French and Portuguese fleet off Vila Franca and the island was occupied by the Spanish. Only when Portugal regained its independence did São Miguel prosper as a trading centre once more. The early crops of wheat, sugar cane and woad were complemented with maize, yams, sweet potatoes and oranges. The export of oranges to England was a great money earner in the 18th century and until 1860, when the trees were destroyed by blight. Since then the farmers have introduced various new crops such as pineapple and tea.

The volcanic nature of the island which destroyed Vila Franca on one hand has contributed to creating an island of outstanding beauty on the other. In the west, the Caldeira das Sete Cidades is the most dramatic of all the Azorean volcanic calderas. A small village has existed for centuries on the crater floor strung along the shores of the twin lakes, one a vivid blue and the other green. To explain how the colour of the waters differ even though they connect, local legend tells that the lakes were formed from the tears of a princess and a shepherd boy forbidden from meeting.

Around the village of Furnas farther east, is a completely different attraction for the visitor, a large area of thermal springs and boiling mud pools. The first American consul to the Azores built a country house nearby, which has now been converted into a hotel. Set in beautiful grounds planted with exotic trees, shrubs and flowers, visitors can sample the warm thermal waters in the hotel's swimming pool. The Furnas area is particularly beautiful in the spring when the azaleas are in flower.

Up in the mountains above Furnas another large lake Lagoa do Fogo lies deep in the crater of an extinct volcano. A small path zigzags down to a sandy beach beside the translucent turquoise waters. Buzzards, after whom the Azores were named, glide on thermals without a motion of their wings. The newly paved road up to the rim of the crater offers splendid views over the island in every direction, while the volcano slopes are deeply grooved by the lava flow and now luxuriantly wooded. A reminder of the nature of the island is the steam pouring out of the ground where a new project is under way to harness the thermal power to generate electricity.

An old narrow cobbled road sunken between hydrangea hedges and towering eucalyptus trees winds magnificently

SÃO MIGUEL

up to the Lombadas valley. The scenery is vivid with green heather bushes and large ferns. The road winds past the old spa of Caldeira de Ribeira, where hot pools bubble away, and eventually reaches the spring at Lombadas where a shed houses the plant for bottling São Miguel's tasty mineral water.

In contrast to the unspoilt interior, the capital Ponta Delgada is a busy city, with the only tall building in the Azores incongruously towering over the attractive 16th century buildings. Originally a small fishing port, its natural harbour soon led to it becoming the main port of the island. It was heavily fortified in the 16th and 17th centuries against the attacks of pirates. The building of the artificial port began in 1861 and the setting up of various industries led to the development of Ponta Delgada as the largest centre in the Azores. As well as being one of the administration centres of the autonomous government, it is also the seat of the University of the Azores.

NAVIGATION

For such a large island, São Miguel is rather lacking in ports and anchorages, so it is not surprising that few venture outside the all weather comfort of Ponta Delgada.

The south coast is sheltered in the summer and there are several small ports well worth a visit, particularly the fishing port of Lagoa. Sailing east from Ponta Delgada along the south coast there is almost continuous ribbon of development. The first conspicuous landmark is the distinctive shape of São Roque, a large rock which lies inshore close to the village of the same name. Within the large bay, of which Ponta Delgada takes up the western half, there are several smaller bays, each with its own beach and adjacent resort, but without any special attractions worth stopping for. There are day anchorages at Caloura and Galera before one reaches Porto Caloura.

After Vila Franca do Campo, the

southeast coast as far as Ponta da Garça is low and featureless. It then starts rising again leading to the spectacular east coast with its towering cliffs. The only possible anchorage in good weather on this coast is at Praia do Lombo Gordo. Continuing anticlockwise around the island, the north coast has several day anchorages off sandy beaches or small ports, but these can only be used in calm weather or when the wind has a southerly component.

The southwest coast is mostly sheer cliffs with narrow strips of stony beaches at their base. There are several places where one can find a day anchorage during settled northeast weather, such as at Feteiras.

LIGHTS

Ponta Delgada breakwater 37°44'.12N 25°39'.40W   Oc R 3s 15m 5M
Porto da Caloura   37°42'.8N 25°29'.8W
Fl W 4s 7m 9M
Vila Franca do Campo 37°42'.8N 25°25'.9W   Fl R 5s 12m 7M
Ponta Garça   37°42'.8N 25°22'.2W
Fl W R 5s 101m W16M R13M
Ribeira Quente   37°43'.9N 25°17'.9W
Iso R 6s 10m 7M
Ponta do Arnel   37°49'.4N 25°08'.2W
Fl W 5s 67m 25M
Povoação   37°44'.7N 25°14'.8W
Oc R 4s 9m 6M
Porto Formoso   37°49'.4N 25°25'.6W
Fl R 4s 6M
Ponta do Cintrão   37°50'.7N 25°29'.4W
Fl(2) W 10s 118m 16M
Rabo de Peixe   37°48'.9N 25°35'.0W
Oc R 3s 9m 6M
Capelas   37°50'.4N 25°41'.2W
Iso R 4s 115m 12M
Bretanha   37°53'.9N 25°45'.3W
Fl W 6s 70m 7M
Mosteiros   37°53'.9N 25°49'.4W
Oc R 3s 10m 6M
Ferraria   37°51'.2N 25°51'.2W
Fl(3) W 20s 107m 27M
Santa Clara   37°43'.9N 25°41'.2W
Fl W 5s 27m 15M

PONTA DELGADA

The majority of yachts visiting São Miguel make their base in the capital Ponta Delgada and explore the rest of this green island by other means of transport.

The town has several imposing churches, palaces and old city houses, including some of the best examples of the Azorean baroque style with white rendered walls, windows and doors being framed by the dark volcanic stone. The large squares and wide pavements paved with black and white mosaic cobbles in intricate design are some of the finest in the Azores. A wide promenade curves from the old fort around the harbour to the new marina and is busy in the evenings when townspeople take a stroll. The building of the marina and swimming pool as well as the planned cafés and restaurants at the eastern end of this promenade provide a social focus that the town previously lacked.

Being by far the largest town in the Azores, many things can be found in Ponta Delgada that are not available in the other islands. It is particularly recommended to stock up here, as the supermarkets have a much better selection than elsewhere.

Approaches

The approaches to Ponta Delgada are straightforward and the town is easily distinguished by a tall building, which sticks up gracelessly into the sky. The port is marked by a long outer breakwater, which, when approaching from the southwest, effectively masks almost all of the town. This breakwater has a red light (occulting 3 secs) at the end, which should not be passed too close when turning into the port as there are some fallen blocks in the water.

A couple of boating accidents in the summer of 1993 has made the Capitania apply stricter rules in the waters adjacent to Ponta Delgada. It is now prohibited to navigate under sail within the immediate port area, i.e. inside the main breakwater,

Ponta Delgada Marina

where one should manoeuvre with utmost caution. It is also prohibited to sail within 300 metres of the shore inside the bay of Ponta Delgada.

The marina is located at the eastern extremity of Ponta Delgada harbour, opposite the end of the main breakwater. The marina is protected by its own smaller breakwater, the end of which is marked by a green flashing light. A number of tetrahedral blocks, used in the construction of the breakwater, have tumbled in the water creating a hazard near the end of the breakwater, which should not be passed too closely.

Formalities

All boats are required to come to the reception quay to clear in with the Guarda Fiscal, whether they are going to stay in the marina or elsewhere. The Guarda Fiscal is on permanent duty at the marina and will clear boats at any time without claiming overtime charges. Policia Maritima (Capitania) also has an office on the reception quay, but its officers are only on partial duty at the marina. It is expected that during the summer they will be there during normal working hours, otherwise the skipper of boats arriving from outside Portugal will have to go to the main Capitania office to obtain the transit log. Boats which have already cleared into the Azores need only see the Guarda Fiscal. After clearance, one will be allocated a berth by the marina office or one can take one of the buoys in the harbour.

Port Facilities

There are about a dozen large red mooring buoys inside the harbour area provided by the Ponta Delgada Port Authority (Junta Autonoma do Porto de Ponta Delgada). In principle, permission to use the moorings should be obtained from the Port Authority office marked 'Exploração' on the main quay. A small daily charge is supposed to be made but in the summer of 1993, the Port Authority did not collect the charges and cruising boats used the moorings without paying. Some crews using the moorings left their dinghies on one of the marina pontoons, which seemed to be tolerated. An alternative is to leave the dinghy at the steps by the swimming area, south of the marina, which is nearer to town and where there are public toilets and cold showers. Dinghies may also be left at the yacht club pontoon, in the northern part of the marina.

Ponta Delgada Marina

This new marina was opened in 1993 and in order to be able to cater for the increasing number of visiting yachts, only 60 of the 110 slips have been allocated to local boat owners, the remaining 50 being reserved for visitors. Modelled on the highly successful marina at Horta, Ponta Delgada Marina offers the usual range of services, such as water and electricity at every slip, hot showers, 24 hour security, all of which are included in the daily fee.

Marina charges will go up in February 1994 by approximately 10 per cent to keep pace with inflation. The approximate charges in escudos for a boat between 10 and 12 metres LOA are as follows: 1,200 (per day), 32,000 (per month), 150,000 (six months), 250,000 (one year). The next category is 12 to 15 metres LOA, for which the charges are approximately the following: 1,500 (per day), 40,000 (per month), 190,000 (six months), 320,000 (one year). There is also a daily charge of 300 escudos per person to cover the use of water, electricity and showers.

Because the opening of the marina had to be rushed for the summer of 1993, some services will only come on stream in time for the next season, such as a fuel dock, service yard and laundry. Also starting in 1994, the marina will be monitoring VHF channel 16 during office hours, which are 0800-1800 seven days a week. The marina is close to all amenities. Marinaçores, Apartado 3, Calheta, 9500 Ponta Delgada, Azores. Tel. 27400, Fax 27300.

Mail can be sent to this address and will be kept for a yacht's arrival. Metered telephone calls can be made from the marina office. The marina office obtains by fax every day a weather forecast for the next 48 hours and, on request, will obtain longer forecasts by fax.

Yacht Club

Clube Naval de Ponta Delgada, Tel. 23005, moved in 1993 to new premises in the marina. Visiting sailors should contact the club secretariat first, after which they are welcome to use its premises, which include a snack bar, indoor swimming pool and gymnasium. One branch of the club is active in scuba diving. Equipment can be hired from the club, which has its own compressor and even a decompression chamber.

Marine Services

The presence of a large fishing fleet as well as a rapidly expanding pleasure boat fleet means that repair facilities are among the best in the Azores. The situation should improve even more once the marina's own boatyard is properly set up. The list below includes all the workshops and specialists used to dealing with yachts, but because of language difficulties it is probably better to ask the marina to contact them. Most addresses are in Ponta Delgada, although some workshops are located out of town.

Boatyards

The marina plans to have its own yard fully operational by 1994. In the absence of a travelift, boats are hoisted by crane and, in order to reduce costs, several owners make arrangements to have their boats lifted out at the same time. The 30 ton crane is supplied by the construction company Alcindo Alves, Tel. 32421, who charges approximately 50,000 escudos for the use. This cost can be shared out among several boats. Until the marina yard becomes operational, owners do their own work, although the marina will call out any specialists if needed.

A boatyard operates in the commercial harbour and is used mainly by local fishing boats. Boats can be slipped, although keeled boats are preferably lifted out by the 25 mobile crane belonging to the Port Authority. The hourly charge for the crane is approximately 15,000 escudos.

Chandleries

MAP, Rua do Mercado 51A, Ponta Delgada, Tel. 25635, Fax 629244. The chandlery is close to the municipal market, three blocks above the marina.

MARINA DE PONTA DELGADA

Under the management of:

FUEL STATION • LAUNDRY • HOT SHOWERS
RESTAURANT • SNACK BAR • NIGHT CLUB

Avenida Infante D. Henrique, Apartado 3 – Calheta
9500 Ponta Delgada Tel: (096) 27400 – Fax (096) 27300

SOL ★ MAR

SUPERMARKET / HYPERMARKET

For all types of fresh produce, food and other supplies. We deliver free of charge to Ponta Delgada Marina

SUPERMERCADO SOL★MAR
AV. INFANTE D. HENRIQUE, 57
PONTA DELGADA, SÃO MIGUEL
TEL: 23735/23717 FAX: 629013

HIPERMERCADO SOL★MAR
ESTRADA DE S. GONÇALO, 223
PONTA DELGADA, SÃO MIGUEL
TEL: 653337 FAX: 653309

It has a small selection of boating equipment, marine paints, outboard engines (Yamaha and Suzuki), marine batteries, fishing and diving gear. It also stocks Portuguese charts of the Azores. Open Monday to Friday 0900-1230, 1400-1830, Saturday 0900-1300.

Honorato Moreira e Monteiro, Estrada Regional, São Roque, Tel. 31124. Located near the fuel station in São Roque, the first village going east from Ponta Delgada, Honorato Moreira has a good selection of Portuguese charts for the Azores, mainland Portugal and the adjacent Atlantic waters. They also hold a stock of equipment and spares, and can obtain essential spares from mainland Portugal.

Diesel Engines

Açornave, Estradinho, Doca, Ponta Delgada, Tel. 22288. The workshop is in the commercial harbour (Doca) and an engineer will come to the boat if called by the marina office.

Outboard Engines

Pereira & Pereira, Avenida Infante Dom Henrique 55, Ponta Delgada, Tel. 26271.

Honorato Moreira e Monteiro, see above.

Transmission Repair

Açornave, see above.

Electrical Repair

Dinis Varão, Avenida Antonio M. Almeida 19, Lagoa, Tel. 92875.

Electronic Repair

Açortrónica Lda, Rua João Moreira 13, Ponta Delgada, Tel. 23592.

J.B.N. Electrónica, Rua Dr João Francisco Sousa 77, Ponta Delgada, Tel. 23781.

Metalwork

Atlantinox, Rua do Mercado 50A, Ponta Delgada. A well equipped workshop next to the market undertakes work in stainless steel and aluminium.

Açornave, see above.

Refrigeration Repair

António Melo, Rua Dr Hermano Medeiros e Camara 77, Capelas, Tel. 98654.

Atlantinox, Rua do Mercado 50A, Ponta Delgada.

Fibreglass Repair

Fibromar, Santa Rosa 3, Fajã Baixo, Lagoa, Tel. 31129.

Honorato Moreira e Monteiro, see above.

Clube Naval de Ponta Delgada, the yacht club can also help out with small repairs.

Woodwork

Mestre Aldeia, Doca, Ponta Delgada, a skilled shipwright working in the boatyard next to the commercial harbour.

Mestre José Maria, a good carpenter who can be contacted via the marina.

Sail Repair

Os Motas, Ponta Delgada, Tel. 35040. They only do repairs.

Fuel

Before the marina has its own fuel station, which is scheduled to open in 1994, fuel can be obtained at the existing GALP station inside the commercial harbour. The station is on the main wharf, close to the root of the breakwater, in the area where the fishing boats are docked. In fact, the fuel dock itself is often occupied by a fishing vessel, so one might have to come alongside to take on fuel, which is preferable to lying alongside the large tyre fenders. The fuel outlet is next to the small blue dock crane. An attendant is available Monday to Friday 0800-1230, 1400-1800. Besides diesel fuel they also exchange standard Portuguese gas bottles.

Gas Filling

Mobil-Gaz, Nordela (near the airport), Tel. 22277, will fill or exchange gas bottles.

J.H.Ornelas, Avenida Infante Dom Henrique, Ponta Delgada, Tel. 22236.

Camping Gaz, Largo de Camões 36, a small shop without a name, near the marina, will exchange Camping Gaz bottles. Also selling diving and fishing equipment.

Diving

Tanks can be filled at the yacht club, Tel. 23005.

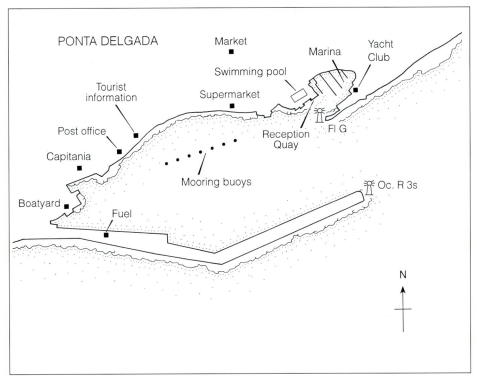

Shore Facilities
Provisioning

Sol Mar, Avenida Infante Dom Henrique, open daily 0900-2300. This excellently stocked supermarket is close to the marina.

Supermercado M. Costa, Rua Eng. José Cordeiro, open daily 0830-2000, is also close to the marina, in the street parallel to the waterfront avenue.

Hipermercado Sol Mar, Tel. 653575, in São Gonçalo, a suburb on the northern outskirts of Ponta Delgada, about 2 km from the marina, is a French style hypermarket which sells everything from tools to shoes, local cheeses to televisions and an excellent selection of fresh fruit, vegetables and meat. The hypermarket is open Monday to Friday 0900-2300, Saturday and Sunday 0830-2030. Large quantities will be delivered free to the marina.

The municipal market is in Rua do Mercado, about three blocks behind the tall building on the waterfront. The market is open Monday, Wednesday, Thursday and Friday 0645-2000, Saturday 0645-1300. Everything is available, from fruit and vegetables to fresh eggs and meat as well as local handicrafts. Locally grown produce, such as pineapples, bananas, melons are very reasonable in season, with prices much lower than anywhere else. There is also a fish market, the selection being much better in the mornings.

Restaurants

Ponta Delgada has a wide selection of restaurants, some of which are close to the marina, such as Marisqueria Açores in Rua Eng. José Cordeiro 20, Tel. 35093, open daily except Mondays from 1200-2400. As the name implies, their speciality is shellfish.

The choice of restaurants for marina users will be even wider after work is finished on the esplanade overlooking the marina, which has been set aside for restaurants and cafés.

Communications

Mail can be sent to the marina c/o Marinaçores, Apartado 3, Calheta, 9500 Ponta Delgada, and will be kept for arrival. Those who do not intend to use the marina may have their mail sent to poste restante (Lista do Correio), 9500 Ponta Delgada.

The post office has four cabins for metered telephone calls and two fax numbers where faxes can be sent or received (27998 and 25084). It is open Monday to Friday 0830-1830, Saturday 0900-1230.

Metered telephone calls can also be made from the marina office.

Weather Forecasts

A weather forecast is posted every day outside the Capitania office, a large building on the waterfront, next to the Navy offices. The Capitania is open Monday to Friday 0900-1230, 1400-1730, but unlike other places, does not have Portuguese charts for sale.

The Meteorological Institute at Nordela, near the airport, Tel. 22922, will provide 7 day forecasts. There is usually a English speaking meteorologist on duty, but the best time to call is from 0600 to 1230 in the morning and from 1330 to 1630 in the afternoon.

The marina office also receives a faxed 48 hour forecast.

Tourist Information

There is an excellent tourist information office on the waterfront, near the post office, Tel. 25152. The office is open Monday to Friday 0900-1900, Saturday 0900-1230, 1400-1730, and Sundays when a cruise ship is in.

Festivals

Santo Cristo dos Milagres, first and second Sunday in May.
Holy Spirit Festivities, end of May.
St. Peter's Horse Calvacades, end of June.

Car Hire

Ilha Verde, Praça 5 de Outubro 12, Ponta Delgada, Tel. 25200, 27301, 27702.

Micauto, Av. Infante Dom Henrique, Ponta Delgada, Tel. 25186 Fax 25186.

Solmar, Centro Comercial Solmar, Ponta Delgada, Tel. 22678.

Autatlantis, Rua das Manaias 65, Largo de Santo André, Ponta Delgada, Tel. 23465, 27146, Fax 27146.

Limota, Rua do Brum 42, Ponta Delgada, Tel. 629338, Fax 629339.

Medical

Hospital: Praça 5 Outubro, Ponta Delgada Tel. 629042.
Emergencies Tel. 22322.

LAGOA

Porto dos Carneiros

A breakwater to the southwest completes the protection of the small Porto dos Carneiros, which occupies the western side of one of the best sheltered bays on the island. The quay has 2 metres depth alongside near the steps at its outer end. There is just sufficient space for a yacht to anchor inside the port. The town of Lagoa lies one kilometre inland. The area around the port caters mainly for the needs of the local fishermen, with several bars and a fish market where the catch is landed every morning. There is a well stocked grocery on the corner of Largo do Porto, selling fresh bread and local produce. It is open Monday to Saturday 0830-2000, and also on Sundays in summer. With an active fishing fleet on its doorstep it is not surprising that one of the best fish restaurants on the island, Restaurante Lota, is located here.

There are no other facilities in the port itself. There is a water tap and hose by the old red light tower, but the light itself is no longer working. Fuel has to be carried by jerrycan either from the Mobil station, about one km up the road to Ponta Delgada, or from the Shell station in the centre of Lagoa.

Determined to attract more yachts to Lagoa and the surrounding area, the Municipal Council intends to build a small marina as part of a hotel development in an area west of the existing fishing port.

To the east of the port is a beautiful swimming area with several deep inlets among the rocks. An attractive bay, with a rocky beach, opens up next, below Lagoa and its distinctive 16th century church. The bay provides a good anchorage in 5 metres on sand, and has the advantage of being closer to town than the fishing port. Next to the church is Marisqueria Regional, an excellent seafood restaurant.

The Vieira Pottery, making blue and white pottery by hand since 1864, is well worth a visit. Open Monday to Friday 0830-1230, 1400-1800, Saturday 0900-1330. In summer, it does not close for lunch. Tel. 92116.

CALOURA

A small resort has sprung up below the village of Água de Pau in this attractive bay east of Ponta Delgada. From the top of a cliff, the new Hotel Caloura overlooks a succession of attractive coves, each with its own rock pool. A good spot for a day anchorage is right under the hotel. The dinghy can be left at the steps used by the swimmers. A better alternative is to anchor in the more protected bay to the west, by the beach. There is a snack bar on the beach and water tap on the road into the village, close to the hotel gates.

GALERA

This is another small resort and possible day anchorage by the headland of the same name (Ponta da Galera). The foreshore is made up of large lava rocks, which have created several narrow inlets but as there are a number of offlying rocks, the area should be approached only in good light.

PORTO CALOURA

This small fishing port, at the mouth of Vale dos Cabaços, lies a couple of miles eastwards of the resort which took its name, possibly causing some confusion. The sparkling white building of a convent standing on the headland immediately to the west of the port makes an excellent landmark. The tiny cove is extremely picturesque and is dwarfed by the huge cliffs which surround it. Leading lights guide boats through a cluster of rocks which surround the small quay, but this has no depth to come alongside in a keeled boat. About twenty boats are pulled up the ramp by

Porto dos Carneiros, Lagoa

Porto Caloura

the fish house where there is also a water tap and hose.

A yacht is best anchored close to the end of the breakwater, which has its own light. The dinghy can be left by the ladder at the end of the quay. The cove is well protected from winds from west through north to east.

There are showers in the public bath house as the small breakwater also encloses a natural pool used by swimmers. There is a snack bar on the road leading up towards the 16th century convent, Nossa Senhora da Conceição, whose church has an exquisite facade decorated in blue and white tiles. Unfortunately the convent is now a private residence and is not open to the public. A special mass is held on the second Sunday in September, the only time when the public is allowed inside.

There are no shops in the small resort and the village of Água de Pau is a long way inland.

VILA FRANCA DO CAMPO

This old town has one of the most attractive main squares anywhere in the Azores. What makes it particularly attractive is the unity of style as well as the beautifully laid out gardens watched with a steady gaze by the bronze statue of the founder of Vila Franca, Gonçalo Vaz Botelho who started the first settlement in 1444. Among the many churches that grace the ancient capital of the island, the Church of São Miguel, overlooking the main square, is as old as the town itself. Particularly noteworthy is its altar which is intricately carved and covered in gold.

The port is surprisingly small and is protected from both east and west by two short breakwaters. The western breakwater runs into a line of rocks which provide additional protection from that direction. There is little depth along the western, curved quay and even by the crane and steps there is only about one metre of depth. The eastern quay is used by boats with deeper draft as it has 2 metres by the first (outer) set of steps. This section is in constant use during the summer by the small ferry which takes people on day trips to Ilhéu de Vila. As there is always some surge inside the port it is probably better to anchor off to the southeast where there are some moorings for the larger fishing boats, the smaller ones being hauled out ashore.

Ilhéu de Vila off the town has a small perfectly round lagoon with an entrance on the northern side. A shallow drafted boat can be taken in at high tide, but most yachts will prefer to anchor off the entrance and explore this pool by dinghy.

Facilities

There is a water tap by the shrine, right below the light, but no other facilities in the port itself.

The fish canning factory above the port, in the yellow buildings, has a well equipped workshop and would help out in an emergency. A shipwright has his small workshop on the waterfront, next

Vila Franca do Campo

Ribeira Quente

to Restaurante O Bravo. The town has a large number of shops. The nearest are in the square, Largo de Bento de Góes, which is at the end of the street leading up from the port. For fuel, a Mobil station, the nearest to the port, is on the far corner of the same square.

Rua Teófilo Braga leads past the Mobil fuel station and along it are most places of interest. A bakery is on Rua da Cadeira Velha, the first turning on the right going towards the centre. The bakery is open Monday to Saturday 0600-2100. The post office is also on Rua Teófilo Braga, on the corner with Rua Visconde da Palmeira. Metered telephone calls can be made and faxes sent and received (Fax 52402). It is open Monday-Friday 0900-1230, 1400-1800.

Supermercado O Cabo do Mar is on the same street. It has the best selection in town and is open Monday to Saturday 0830-1900, Sunday 0830-1200. Farther up and close to the main square is the municipal market, with several stalls selling fresh local produce and also local handicrafts, including pottery. The market is open Monday to Saturday 0700-1800, Sunday 0700-1200.

To see a local potter at work, one should follow the signs to Olaria (pottery). An old potter has a small pottery and kiln on the waterfront producing jugs and other utensils. The unpainted reddish pottery is typical of Vila Franca, as opposed to the more refined blue and white pottery of Lagoa.

RIBEIRA QUENTE

The fast flowing river that gave its name to the small village flows into the sea immediately to the east of the new breakwater. Both the scenic road leading up to Furnas and the new breakwater were financed as part of a European Community project. It is possible to come alongside the quay which has at least 2 metres depth on its western (inner) side, but one should keep as close to the outer end as possible and not go as far as the steps where there are a couple of large rocks on the bottom. One can anchor as close to the breakwater as practical, the bottom is sand and small rocks. An alternative anchorage can be found off the beach in front of the village.

The fish freezing plant, the large building close to the ramp, has a well equipped workshop. There is a water tap and toilets in a small building on the road leading up along the river. A public telephone is farther up the same road, which goes to Furnas, and also the Minimercado Mini 15, Tel. 54460, which has a café open all day from 0800 until 2300 if there are clients in the café. The waterfront road leads westwards to the larger part of the village clustered around the beach.

POVOAÇÃO

The site of the first settlement on the island commands a beautiful spot in a verdant valley, but neither its shore nor the tiny port are of any merit. The port itself is nothing more than a short quay and small ramp. Another European Community project is in progress here in an area east of the existing quay to reclaim land in the form of a breakwater which will hold a restaurant and swimming area. Presumably it will also add protection to the recommended anchorage in the small indentation southeast of the town.

The small town has a number of shops, with the best supermarket in the square by the church. Supermercado João Luis Mendoça is open Monday to Friday 0830-1200, 1330-1800, Saturday 0830-1230. The nearest and only fuel station is Shell, located 100 metres from the main square on the road leading eastwards out of town.

PRAIA DO LOMBO GORDO

A day anchorage in spectacular surroundings off the best beach on the island overlooked by towering cliffs. A stop is only feasible in southwest to northwest winds, or better still, in calm weather and no swell. Anchor close to the beach in 5 metres on sand with good holding. The only building ashore has showers and a snack bar.

NORDESTE

The spectacular scenery continues all along the east coast. A small and relatively well protected bay at the foot of the light on Ponta do Arnel has allowed the building of a tiny port dwarfed by the huge cliffs that surround it. The bay offers protection from southwest to north winds through west. There is anchoring depth close to the quay and the dinghy can be taken to the steps. A few boats are hauled out on the ramp. A very steep road climbs up first to the lighthouse, then to the village of Nordeste.

PORTO FORMOSO

True to its name ('beautiful port'), this small port occupies a beautiful setting amongst banks covered in flowers of all colours, blue hydrangeas, red and gold cannas, white daisies and pink roses. The port itself is in fact a sandy beach with the boats hauled ashore. The bay is protected in winds from east through south to west. The village, however, does not live up to its name with the exception of its church. There is a grocery shop (Minimercado Beira Mar) in the main street, but little else.

PRAIA DOS MOINHOS

Only one mile west of Porto Formoso are two equally beautiful beaches named after some windmills which no longer exist. There is good anchoring in either bay, with the western one being closer to the resort with shops and cafés in the one street village.

PORTO DE SANTA IRIA

Tucked away behind Ponta do Cintrão in one of the most attractive settings on the island, the tiny port offers good protection in winds from east through south to west. Protection is increased by a cluster of large rocks. There is a clear way between the offlying rocks to anchor in 6 to 8 metres in the middle of the southern bay, where a handful of fishing boats are hauled up the steep ramp. What looks like a quay is in fact a swimming platform. An alternative anchorage can be found in the northern bay, which is equally well protected. A 2 km walk leads into Ribeirinha.

RIBEIRA GRANDE

The largest town on the north coast has no port, only a swimming complex which had been built among a group of rocks to create two large pools. Although one may be able to anchor in the wide bay, this old town which contains many attractive old buildings, churches and chapels, is best visited by land.

RABO DO PEIXE

There is a small quay in the northeast corner of a bay offering protection from east through south to southwest. The village of the same name is spread out on top of the surrounding cliffs. This is

Porto de Santa Iria

the busiest and most prosperous fishing port on the north coast. There are several shops in and around the square by the main church.

SÃO VICENTE

A short quay with insufficient depth for keeled boats alongside it serves the village of São Vicente, with local boats pulled up on the nearby beach. There are several rocks in the approaches making a stop hard to justify. This small, undistinguished port used to be one of the busiest whaling centres in the Azores. The old whaling factory buildings have now fallen into disrepair, although there is a plan to turn them into a whaling museum. Four of the fastest sailing whalers are still kept inside the old factory. Nearby one can see the black stone cottages of the whalers, a community which was still active in the early 1970s before the international moratorium on the hunting of whales spelt the death of their trade. Large number of whales are still seen in the area, which in the past were observed from the tower on the nearby Morro das Capelas headland.

CAPELAS

Sheer cliffs make for a dramatic setting for this well protected bay, which gives shelter in winds from east through south to west. One can anchor close to the quay in 5 to 6 metres, on a sand and rock bottom. A steep climb leads into the village of Capelas which spreads

Capelas

eastwards along the main coastal road. Along that road one can find most of the things one needs. On the corner of the narrow lane leading up from the port and Rua do Cruzeiro is the village bakery. Further along towards the centre is a small grocery. The post office is farther along this main road.

MOSTEIROS

The shape of a large offlying rock, which looks like a house or, with a little imagination, a monastery, has given the name to the nearby point and village. Porto de Mosteiros lies at the head of a deep and narrow inlet protected from all directions except west. There is a small quay and ramp, although there is no depth alongside the quay, which has a light on it. A clear passage through the rocky sides of the bay leads to the ramp, where local boats are hauled ashore. Yachts should anchor in the middle of the bay where the depth is approximately 7 to 8 metres. There is a water tap at the top of the ramp, but otherwise no amenities in the small port. All shops are in the village which spreads to the north and east. Its centre is close to the port, with a grocery in the square by the church, behind the Mar Azul restaurant. Mosteiros is known as the best place on São Miguel for seafood and Mar Azul specialises in local shellfish dishes.

South of Mosteiros there are two deep bays, the northern one providing better protection in northerly winds through east to south. There are several offlying rocks, all clearly visible. The southern bay is more scenic, with two tusk like vertical rock stacks guarding the entrance into the bay. There are several rocks to the northwest, so the area should only be entered in good light and settled weather.

CANDELARIA

A small quay and ramp are used by a handful of fishing boats from the village of Candelaria, which lies about one kilometre inland.

TERCEIRA

The fine natural harbour on the south coast of Terceira was a major factor in the prominence of this island in the history of the Azores. Terceira, meaning third in Portuguese, was the third island to be discovered, hence its name. After discovery, it was quickly settled by Portuguese and Flemish settlers and in 1450 its Captaincy was granted to the Fleming Jácome de Bruges. The town of Angra, which sprang up around this harbour, soon became the most important in the Azores and until 1832 was the archipelago's capital.

By 1500 Angra had many fine mansions, churches and paved streets and was a favourite port of call for Portuguese caravels returning from Africa. Vasco da Gama stopped on his way back from India in 1499 and Azorean sailors departed from Angra on expeditions to Newfoundland and Greenland. A Terceiran, João Fernandez Labrador, sailing on Cabot's second transatlantic voyage gave his name to the land of Labrador.

Terceirans were heavily involved in the politics and history of the Azores, Terceira being the last centre of resistance to the Spanish invasion. The first attempt by the Spanish to conquer the island resulted in their defeat at the hands of the Terceirans in the battle of Salgra, a monument to which overlooks the beach at Salgra Bay. During the Spanish occupation the island became a port of call for the galleons returning from the New World laden with gold and silver. It was the Spaniards who built the fort of São João Baptista to protect Angra and the port rebuffed attacks from such renowned privateers as Sir Francis Drake.

Terceira was also involved in the politics of the 19th century, supporting the liberal cause and becoming the main base for the liberal forces, who established a Regency in Angra. It was from Terceira in 1832 that the expedition left for mainland Portugal, which led eventually to the establishment of a new constitution. It was for the bravery of the citizens of Angra during this civil war that the town was granted the title "Heroísmo" by the Queen of Portugal.

Since that time, the role of Angra do Heroísmo has gradually diminished with the ascendency of Ponta Delgada. In some way this has been compensated for by the building of the large airport, which has opened up a new dimension for the island. Built by the British in 1943, it was given to the Portuguese after the war. It is now the principal international airport serving the Azores. US forces maintain a base here as well as the Portuguese Air Command of the Azores and it is an important part of the NATO defence system, especially as a mid-Atlantic refuelling base. This military and communications aspect can be seen on all the high points of the island, which bristle with antennae and satellite dishes, as well as gun emplacements and other installations left over from the Second World War.

The highest point is the volcanic cone and crater of Santa Barbara, over 1000 metres high, where the road winds up through forests of cryptomerias to the bare summit carpeted with springy moss, heather and tiny flowers. On a clear day one can look across to Pico and São Jorge in one direction and down to the town of Angra in the other. There are equally magnificent views at the opposite end of the island at Serra do Cume, overlooking Praia da Vitória and the northeast of the island.

The interior of the island is surprisingly deserted, with virtually no houses, only herds of black and white cattle grazing in rolling green fields. The large number of cattle on the island gives a clue to a distinctive tradition special to Terceira, that of bullfighting.

The human population of Terceira is concentrated in the towns and villages strung like a ribbon around the coastline.

Terceira is certainly an island of contrasts, from the black volcanic rocks and pools off the north coast near Biscoitos to the eucalyptus forest at Serreta or miles of hydrangea banked hedgerows flanking the lanes which crisscross the centre of the island. Every village and town has a distinctive Espírito Santo chapel, which is usually colourfully decorated and painted in contrast to the white village houses. The sense of community is very strong on Terceira and these Espírito Santo festivities are associated with giving food to the needy. In summer the weekends appear to be one fiesta after another.

NAVIGATION

Angra do Heroísmo on the south coast and Praia da Vitória on the east coast are the two main ports. The bay at Angra is overlooked by the distinctive Monte Brasil and the town is one of the most attractive in the Azores. Praia da Vitória is a less attractive town, but its bay is protected by two long breakwaters giving protection from all directions. It is also conveniently close to the airport at Lajes if crew are flying in or out.

Between the two main ports there are several bays, indentations and small ports along the south and east coasts, which are worth visiting when sailing between Angra and Praia. The north coast, like that of other islands, is more exposed to the weather and can only be visited in stable weather conditions. There is, however, beautiful scenery all along this north coast with jagged black lava rocks spiking up and, on the west coast, dramatic cliffs and bays. Continuing in an anticlockwise direction there are a few anchorages on the southwest coast and, close to Angra, the fishing port of São Mateus.

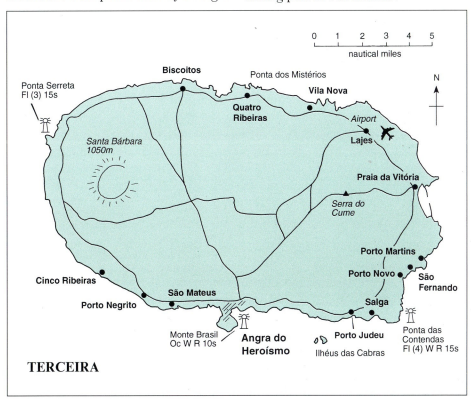

TERCEIRA

Angra do Heroísmo

LIGHTS

Monte Brasil 38°38'.6N 27°13'.1W
Oc W R 10s 22m 12M
Porto Pipas (Angra) 38°39'.1N 27°13'.0W
Fl G 3s 15m 6M
Porto Judeu 38°38'.9N 27°07'.1W
Fl W 3s 28m 7M
Contendas 38°38'.6N 27°05'.1W
Fl(4) W R 15s 54m 23M
São Fernando 38°40'.6N 27°03'.9W
Oc R 3s 6m 6M
Praia da Vitória
South Breakwater 38°43'.2N 27°03'.0W
Fl R 3s 8M
North Breakwater 38°43'.6N 27°03'.1W
Iso G 1s 12m 5M
Vila Nova 38°46'.9N 27°08'.5W
Iso W 6s 11m 9M
Biscoitos 38°48'.0N 27°15'.6W
Oc W 6s 14m 9M
Serreta 38°46'.0N 27°22'.5W
Fl(3) W 15s 96m 21M
Cinco Ribeiras 38°40'.6N 27°19'.8W
Fl W 6s 23m 10M
São Mateus 38°39'.3N 27°16'.1W
Iso W R 6s 12m W10M R7M

ANGRA DO HEROÍSMO

Guarded by Monte Brasil and massive fortresses, the town of Angra do Heroísmo curves around the bay, alive with colour and elegant facades. The first Azorean town to become a city, Angra do Heroísmo had its heyday in the 16th century. During this era, the town was planned with straight streets on a grid in Renaissance manner and many splendid houses, churches and public buildings were constructed. The historical completeness of the town has been recognised by UNESCO who have put Angra on their World Heritage list.

The city has survived in spite of many catastrophes, man-made and natural. In the battles with the Spanish it was ransacked, later to be attacked by both Sir Francis Drake and the Earl of Essex and finally bombarded before being regained by the Portuguese. More recently Angra was hit by a severe earthquake on New Year's Day 1980. Many of the old buildings were damaged and restoring them is still going on.

Today Angra do Heroísmo is one of the administrative centres of the Azores and part of the University is based there.

There are many vantage points to view this pretty town, such as the obelisk in memory of King Pedro IV's visit, which stands high above the town, or from Monte Brasil, over 200 metres high and topped by a cross and British gun emplacements from the Second World War kept in mint condition by the Angra Museum. There are ramparts all around Monte Brasil and built into the hillside is the São João Baptista castle. Built by the Spanish in the 16th century it houses a palace, church and modern day garrison inside its massive walls. One of the best views, however, is from the terrace of the yacht club at sunset when the colours are turning on the old buildings and walls around the bay.

The city has many interesting buildings from the elegant Town Hall to the gothic cathedral, its plain stone and panelled wood ceiling a contrast to the embellishments of the usual Azorean baroque. The streets are narrow, steep and cobbled, the pavements of mosaics and the town houses painted vivid colours with intricate wrought iron work on the balconies and under the eaves, windows outlined in different colours. Some of the houses of the old noble families are palatial, such as that of the Bettencourts, which is now the Public Library. Modern shop interiors are hidden behind old facades, yet in some the solid wooden counters and old-style display cabinets belong to another era.

Approaches

The 200 metre high peninsula of Monte Brasil is the best landmark for Angra do Heroísmo, while the two rocky offshore islets Ilhéus das Cabras are a useful indication by day and should be given a wide berth at night as they are not lit. If approaching from the west, the conspicuous church at São Mateus will be passed before Monte Brasil is rounded and Angra comes into view. Porto das Pipas and the quay where the ferry docks is on the starboard side, while tucked under the cliffs on the port side is the Clube Náutico (Yacht Club). The mooring buoys available for yachts are strung out between the club and the large grey and white church with onion shaped domes on its two towers on the northern shore of the bay.

Formalities

As soon as possible after arrival one should report to the Guarda Fiscal, whose office is in Patio de Alfandega (Customs Quay), the small quay in front of the distinctive onion domed church. This office is open 24 hours. There is also a Guarda Fiscal substation in Porto das Pipas, which may be more convenient depending on where the boat is moored.

Port Facilities

A number of moorings have been laid by the Port Authority (Junta Autonoma do Porto de Angra do Heroísmo) and these can be used free of charge by visitors. Their only drawback is that the large red metal spheres tend to hit the boat if the wind drops or blows against the tide. The solution is to try and tie the boat on as short a line as possible to restrict the scope of the buoy. This means almost lifting the buoy out of the water, which will cause some chafe in the continuous movement, so one should either use a sacrificial line or a length of chain shackled to the ring on the buoy.

The dinghy can be left either at Customs Quay in the small basin in front of the Guarda Fiscal building, which is close to the centre of town and all amenities, or at the yacht club, on the southwest side of the bay. Depending on where one intends to leave the dinghy, one should try to pick a mooring closer either to the town or the yacht club.

There are plans to build a marina in Angra and bearing in mind the determined character of its citizens and the pressures exerted by its sailing community, this is probably going to become a reality in the near future. If so, the marina will be built close to the centre, as are those in Horta and Ponta

Delgada, and will incorporate the small basin at Customs Quay.

Porto das Pipas

The commercial port of Angra has been superseded by the port of Praia da Vitória and is used much less by large ships than in the past. Much of the port area is taken up by local pleasure craft which are moored fore and aft on moorings provided by the Port Authority. Visitors may come alongside the quay, which is rather high for yachts and there are only a small number of access ladders. Also, one should try and position the yacht between the large tyre fenders, which may be easier on the west side where part of the quay has been left free. The Port Authority has a fixed crane on the inner quay used by smaller craft. A larger mobile crane can be ordered for those who wish to be lifted out.

There is a water outlet near the crane. There is a small snackbar on the quay, toilets and showers by the side of the large shed. There are several small workshops in the warehouses on the south side, including a new chandlery (Nautaçor) and a shipwright building sailing dinghies. There are more mechanical workshops on the road leading into town (Avenida Infante D. Henrique). As there is no fuel available in the port, this has to be carried in jerrycans from the Mobil station at the first roundabout going up from the port.

Yacht Club

The club building is quite distinctive on the southwest shore of the bay under

Porto das Pipas

the ramparts and slightly out of town. The club monitors VHF channel 16 (working channel 11) when the bar is open (daily 0900-2300). The club restaurant serves lunches and dinners and is open daily, except Mondays when it serves hot snacks only. International metered telephone calls can be made from the bar. Mail will be held in the club office if it is marked 'yacht in transit'. Clube Náutico de Angra do Heroísmo, Rua Dr Corte Real, Tel 23300.

The club, which enjoys one of the most beautiful settings of any yacht club, is extremely welcoming to visitors, who can use its facilities free of charge, including the hot showers in the club building. There is another set of cold showers below the club house where there is also a water tap with a hose long enough to reach the quay by the crane. It is possible to come alongside the high quay by the crane where there is a minimum depth of 3 metres. There is a metal ladder going up the high quay. Arrangements to come alongside should be made with the yacht club as the boom of the crane has to be turned away so as not to touch the rigging. If moored on one of the buoys or anchored in the bay, the dinghy can be left at the club, by the steps below the crane. The yacht club should be contacted if help is needed with any repair jobs.

Marine Services

Chandleries

Nautaçor, Porto das Pipas. A new establishment located at the western end of the warehouse on the main quay with a small but expanding range of nautical equipment.

Adriano Figueirido, an English speaking member of the yacht club, is a good contact as he supplies other club members with equipment, charts, etc. He can be contacted at the bank where he works, Caixa Economica Açoreana, Rua Direita 143, Tel. 24324.

Charts

Atlantilivro, Rua Barcelos 14, Tel. 27648. Small selection of charts and

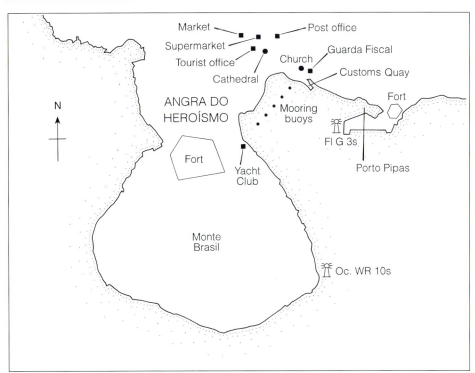

books on the Azores.

Diesel Engines

E.V.T. (Empresa de Viação Terceirense), Rua Dr Sousa Meneses 15, Tel. 27001.

Auto Bacalhau, Careira Cavalos 8-10, Tel. 22444.

Outboard Engines

Stand Sachs, Rua Dr Francisco Silva, Tel. 25702. Agent for Yamaha, Tohatsu.

Auto Bacalhau, see above.

Electrical Repair

João Maurça, contact via yacht club.

Electronic Repair

Electronaves, Rua Canos Verdes 87, Tel. 23409.

Refrigeration Repair

Equipaçor, Rua Canos Verdes 51, Tel. 23311.

Fibreglass Repair

Lourenço Alves, Porto das Pipas, workshop next to the Guarda Fiscal office.

Woodwork

Carpintaria João Gorgita, Porto das Pipas.

Metalworking

Mestre Gil, Porto das Pipas, a skilled metal worker who has a small workshop close to Porto das Pipas, undertakes good quality metal work, fabrication and welding.

Hydraulics and Transmission

E.V.T. see above.

Liferaft Service

Capitania do Porto, Forte São Sebastião, Tel. 22051.

Rigging

Loja Nildo Neves, Rua da Sé 176, Tel. 22466.

Diving

The yacht club has its own compressor and will fill tanks for visitors. The club also rents out diving equipment.

Fuel

This has to be brought in jerrycans from one of the stations in town, but as all are rather far, one would need a car or taxi to take them either to the yacht club or Customs Quay.

Gas (LPG)

Gas bottles (butane) can be filled or

exchanged at a station on Rua Jacinto Candido, close to Porto das Pipas.

Shore Facilities

Provisioning

Armazéns Zeferino, Rua da Sé 110, Tel. 22639, open Monday to Friday 0800-1900, Saturday 0800-1300 is the nearest supermarket and has a good selection of fresh produce, tinned food as well as a fresh meat counter.

A small grocery, on the corner of Rua das Minhas Terras and Rua Direita, close to the Guardia Fiscal building, is the closest to the recommended anchorage. It has a good selection of everything, including fresh fruit and vegetables. Open Monday to Friday 0800-2100, Saturday 0800-2000, Sunday 0900-1300.

Guarita Supermarket, Rua Guarita, is only convenient if moored in Porto das Pipas.

The municipal market, Mercado Duque de Bragança, is in the square of the same name, close to the main thoroughfare, Rua da Sé. The market is open Monday to Friday 0600-1600, Saturday 0700-1400. There are several stalls and small shops, butchers shops selling fresh meat and home made sausages, as well as a fish market which is best visited early in the morning.

Communications

The post office is off the main shopping street on the corner of Rua do Palacio and Rua da Esperança. It is open Monday to Friday 0830-1830 and Saturday 0900-1230. Metered calls can be made

Porto Judeu

from here and faxes received and sent. Fax 25084. Metered calls can also be made from the yacht club.

Restaurants

Restaurante Melo, Rua das Minhas Terras, close to Customs Quay, is a small and reasonably priced restaurant. It serves one of the local specialities, the beef stew *alcatra regional*.

Beira Mar, Rua São João, excellent food and service on a terrace overlooking the harbour.

Laundry

Lavandaria la Suprema, Rua do Santo Espírito.

The yacht club will install two washing machines in 1994.

Car Hire

Angrauto, Rua Frei das Chagas 14, Tel. 25585.

Auto Turística Escobar, Rua Serpa Pinto 17, Tel. 24222.

Ilha 3, Rua de Lisboa 22, Tel. 23115.

Medical

Hospital: Barreiro, Angra do Heroísmo, Tel. 22121.

Tourist information

Rua Rio Janeiro, open Monday to Friday 0900-1230, 1400-1730.

The most important local festival is São João (24 June), two weeks of music, bullfights and yacht races.

PORTO JUDEU

This surprisingly small port serves a large community. The deep and narrow inlet, almost indistinguishable among the high cliffs, has been provided with a small quay with two sets of steps. There is a watertap up the ramp, by the refrigeration plant. The nearest shop is in the main street, Mercado Flor da Dia, with several more shops in the surrounding streets. The Guarda Fiscal building is in Rua do Porto, which is in fact the next street to the one leading down to the port.

BAIA DE SALGA

The scene of a sea battle in 1581 when the Terceirans repulsed the Spaniards, this bay is now a favourite

Praia da Vitória

weekend spot among locals. The small bay is well protected in northerly winds. There is a small quay next to a tidal rock pool at the head of the bay. There is anchoring depth in the bay and the dinghy can be landed at the steps in the quay. A small café overlooks the bay and there is a campsite nearby.

PORTO NOVO

This small but busy port is used by the fishermen of Porto Martins. There is a short quay, with sufficient depth to come alongside, although the space is usually taken up by local boats. There is a watertap up the ramp.

PORTO DE SÃO FERNANDO

The small fishing port is in a narrow inlet with its own short quay and ramp. There is no depth to come alongside the quay, but there is a good anchoring spot nearby. The inlet is well protected from the north by the nearby headland and offers protection right around to winds from the southwest. There is water at the fisheries building on the south side and a grocery shop on the main road of the nearby village.

PORTO MARTINS

An attractive holiday resort set around a bay protected in southwest through west to north winds. There is a small quay on the south side, mostly used by swimmers since a new port was built further south, aptly called Porto Novo.

PRAIA DA VITÓRIA

The second largest town on Terceira, Praia da Vitória was a prosperous town in the 15th and 16th centuries as seen by the large and impressive gothic church founded by the first Captain of Terceira, Jácome de Bruges. Old houses with picturesque verandas line the narrow streets around the main square where the 16th century Town Hall has a typical Azorean facade.

It was the role played during the civil wars, when the town supported the liberal cause and resisted the attempted landing of 21 ships of the absolutist fleet, which resulted in the title *da Vitória* being given to the town. Praia means 'beach' in Portuguese and it is easy to see how the town got its name, as a wide sandy beach curves around the bay in front of the town.

The bay has been enclosed by two long breakwaters, the southern basin being the commercial port, while the northern basin is used by fishermen and other small craft.

Port Facilities

The northern basin is much closer to the town. It is a busy fishing port full of local boats, leaving no space to come alongside, although if there were a space free one could come either to the southern part of the quay or on its inside. The best solution is to anchor as close to the quay as possible, but out of the way of the traffic, and take the dinghy to the inner quay. The small basin formed by the quay is rather dirty and full of small fishing boats. The port is a hive of activity with fishermen working on their boats, painting and carrying out repairs. There is a watertap on the quay but no other facilities whatsoever. The nearest fuel station is GALP, on the waterfront close to the centre, open Monday to Friday 0830-1830, Saturday 0800-1200. They also exchange gas bottles.

The area east of the inner breakwater, by the beach, is prohibited landing as it belongs to the Portuguese Air Force who have a base there. Because of the long fetch inside the large harbour, a strong south or southwest wind would make the chop on the northern side rather uncomfortable. In such conditions it would be advisable to move to the southern part of the port, in the commercial area, where one can either anchor or tie up to the massive quay. The high quay is fronted with large tyre fenders which make it rather difficult to tie up a yacht. The large port and the adjacent installations are little used. There is water on the quay but no other facilities. A set of manned gates give access to the quay, which may be used by visiting yachts, the main inconvenience being the distance from town, which is approximately 3 km away.

Facilities

For such a busy fishing port, repair facilities are rather disappointing, presumably because the fishermen manage to do all their own running repairs, while for anything more complicated one has to go to Angra.

There is a good woodworking shop locally, Carpintaria João Alvarino, Tel. 52189. The yacht club (Clube Náutico de Praia da Vitória) is close to the port, but is only open on weekends. The club has its own diving compressor.

There are several small grocery shops and a new supermarket in Rua Gervásio Lima, close to the police station. The post office is in the main square, Largo F. Ornelas, and metered telephone calls can be made there.

Tourist Information is in Rua Anicelo d'Ornelas. A local festival takes place from 5 to 15 August.

VILA NOVA

This deep and well protected bay on the north coast offers shelter in northwest to east winds through south. There is only an old stone ramp at its head with all boats pulled up ashore. It is a long walk into the village of same name.

PONTA DOS MISTÉRIOS

This is one of the most attractive coastal areas on the island. There are bays on both sides of Ponta dos Mistérios, the one to the west offering better protection in northeast to west winds through south.

QUATRO RIBEIRAS

The southwest corner of the wide bay west of Ponta das Quatro Ribeiras, below the village of the same name, is deeply indented offering the best protection in winds from east through south to west. The sea shelves towards the rocky beach and there is anchoring depth close to where a few boats are hauled ashore.

Westwards, towards Ponta dos Biscoitos, the lava rock coast is indented with several deep inlets making for dramatic scenery.

BISCOITOS

This small port is set among black lava rocks. There is a short quay on the east side and a ramp with a large number of boats pulled ashore. There are no facilities in the port, except a watertap on the ramp, but the large fishing community has been pressing for a better port and work on it will begin in 1994 with help from the European Community. A café and restaurant overlooks the port and there is a bathing area nearby used by swimmers. The nearby village has a number of shops.

This entire stretch of coast has countless protected coves and rock pools.

PONTA DA SERRETA

The light on Ponta da Serreta marks the westernmost point of the island. There are bays on both sides of the high headland, overlooked by steep cliffs several hundred metres high. The northern bay, Baía Pequena, offers better protection, especially in southwest to east winds through south. One can anchor in its southeast corner by a small rocky beach, but there is no access ashore. The fishing is reputed to be excellent, especially spearfishing around the rocks and in the underwater caves.

CINCO RIBEIRAS

This fishing village on the southwest coast has a small port tucked away among the rocks. A conspicuous chapel on a headland west of the port provides a useful landmark. The port has a short quay and ramp, with several boats pulled up ashore. There is anchoring depth close inshore and one can land at the steps on the quay or at the ramp. A snack bar overlooks the port, which in summer is used mostly by swimmers.

PORTO NEGRITO

The quay of this former whaling station has been converted for use by swimmers, with the old quay being linked to the surrounding rocks to form a tidal pool. The old fort as well as the buildings and installations ashore are now the site of a pub disco, the Vida Maritima. The deep inlet provides good protection, but when approaching it from the southeast, one should avoid a group of rocks over which the seas are breaking by favouring the west side of the inlet when entering.

PORTO SÃO MATEUS

This busy fishing port is overlooked by an attractive twin-towered church which provides an excellent landmark. The port consists of two basins, the northern one being used by smaller boats. There are two moorings for visiting boats (marked JAPAH) and, as space for anchoring is limited, it is better to try

São Mateus

and use one of these moorings. The southern basin has a quay where it is possible to come alongside, although reaching it past the moored boats, which tie up with long lines to the shore, may not be easy. The only reason to try and come alongside is to get fuel, this being the only place on Terceira where fuel can be loaded directly from a pump ashore. There is a GALP station on the quay, which is not normally manned but an attendant will be sent by the company if requested. Smaller amounts of fuel can be bought in jerrycans from the Shell station in the main road.

There is no water on the quay, only a tap on the ramp, and no other facilities in the port itself. In spite of the large number of local fishing boats, there are no adequate repair facilities in São Mateus itself and for any repair jobs one has to go into nearby Angra. There are several small bars and shops overlooking the port and facilities may improve once work is completed on the large building in the centre of the port.

CAIS DE SILVEIRA

The nearest bay west of the capital Angra offers excellent protection from the southeast through north to west. If there is too much swell in Angra due to southeast winds, this attractive bay can provide a good alternative for awaiting a change in the weather. The bay is overlooked by the São João Baptista fortress on Monte Brasil. The easiest access ashore is up a set of white painted steps on the east side leading up to the road below the fortress.

GRACIOSA

Graciosa is the least mountainous of the Azores, with rolling hills and valleys, green and fertile in the 'gracious' way of its name. Due to the fact that most of the island can be cultivated, it has always been prosperous. Cattle raising is the mainstay of the economy, but maize is a major crop and wine is also produced commercially.

It is not sure exactly when the island was discovered and appears to have been settled from nearby Terceira, although by 1486 a town charter had been granted to the main settlement of Santa Cruz. Although suffering its share of attacks by pirates in those early years, generally Graciosa has had a quieter history than the bigger islands, maybe because it has always been a rural island, its population concentrating on agriculture and cattle raising.

No island in the Azores can escape its volcanic origins and Graciosa is no exception, with sulphur springs inside the caldera at the southwest of the island. A tunnel takes the road right into the crater floor, which is covered with grass like an Alpine meadow, surrounded by the wooded green slopes of the crater. 177 steps cut into the rockface spiral down to the cavern Furna do Enxofre, a huge grotto lit by filtered light through several chimney-like openings. The smell of sulphur lingers in the air as hot springs bubble between yellow sculpted rocks. At one side of the cavern is a small lake, on which one used to be able to row in a small boat, but now is out of bounds following a fatal accident when two men were overcome with fumes after taking the boat without permission into the deepest reaches of the cavern. The cavern is open every day from 1100 to 1600 except on Thursdays.

The sulphurous mineral water has been tamed in the spa at Carapacho on the south coast. Reputed to be good for rheumatism and dermatological disorders, the old spa buildings have recently been renovated and were reopened in 1993. There are about 20 individual bathrooms where for around 1000 escudos one can relax in the tingling warm water, while the sand runs out on the 15 minute hourglass, the maximum time recommended. Medical consultations are available.

The capital Santa Cruz was built around a small fishing harbour now little used. The town is pleasantly laid out with white and pink washed houses around two small ponds and a tree lined square. An excellent view of the town and surrounding countryside is from Monte da Ajuda behind the town, where three chapels are situated, the oldest, four hundred years old, being fortified like a castle.

A similar chapel, lit up at night, is on the hill overlooking Praia, a small town with attractive windmills on its outskirts. The old inner harbour is minuscule, but a new breakwater has created the best protected port on the island.

The windmills of Graciosa are quite distinctive with red onion shaped domes like Russian Orthodox churches. They are scattered throughout the island, but are no longer in use, although some have been converted into holiday homes. The villages are neat and tidy, with small white washed houses topped by unusually large wedge-shaped chimneys. On the narrow lanes, donkeys pull carts with solid wooden wheels and one wonders if the twentieth century has passed Graciosa by.

Santo Cristo is the island's main fiesta and takes place mainly in Santa Cruz in August, starting on the second Sunday of the month and finishing on the following Saturday. The list of entertainment is varied and usually includes a bullfight.

NAVIGATION

In contrast to some of the other Azorean islands, there are various islets and rocks off the coasts of Graciosa, which must be paid attention to when sailing close inshore. The best protected port and most favoured by yachts is at Praia on the east coast. The harbour of Santa Cruz, in the north eastern corner of the island, has limited protection and the prevailing swell rolls in even in calm conditions. Local sailors keep their boats in the better sheltered bay Cais da Barra south of Santa Cruz. If sailing up from Praia one should keep half a mile off the coast to avoid all dangers. There is a group of dangerous rocks off the northeast point at Cais da Barra and several more offlying rocks on the way into Santa Cruz, the furthest being nearly half a mile out.

The rest of the island offers little in the way of anchorages, although sailing along the coast provides some dramatic views where the cliffs are often colourfully striated and there are beautiful day anchorages at both Porto Afonso and Folga in settled weather. The most distinctive offshore rock close by the lighthouse at Ponta da Barco is in the shape of a whale. Whale Rock is part of the rim of a crater, the rest forming the steepsided cliffs, a splash of red and ochre stripes on black rock standing out dramatically against the azure water of the small bay.

LIGHTS

Santa Cruz   39°05'.3N 28°00'.6W
Fl R 5s 14m 7M
Praia   39°03'.1N 27°58'.0W
Fl G 3s 16m 9M
Carapacho   39°00'.8N 27°57'.4W
Fl(2) W 10s 191m 15M
Folga   39°01'.5N 27°58'.1W
Fl W 5s 31m 4M
Ponta da Barca 39°05'.6N 28°03'.0W
Fl W 7s 71m 20M

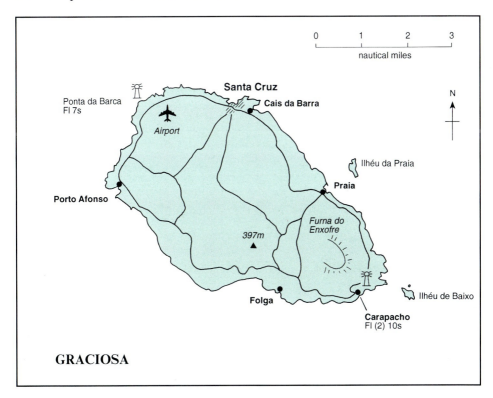

GRACIOSA

SANTA CRUZ

This small attractive town has a large central square shaded by tall pine trees and elms, where two old cattle reservoirs form decorative ponds. Nearby the four hundred year old parish church contains six 16th century painted panels by an unknown artist which are considered masterpieces of early Portuguese art and are known as the Graciosa Panels.

One old house in the town has been turned into an Ethnographic Museum, open Monday to Friday 0900-1230, 1400-1730. The collection has concentrated on preserving objects of domestic use from Graciosa's past, including furniture, family albums, kitchen utensils, even a hat collection. Perhaps the most valuable item is a 17th century wooden statue of Santa Barbara. Another lady greets one at the museum entrance; the figurehead of the schooner *Julia* wrecked close to Praia in 1906. On the ground floor are farming tools, wine presses, animal driven mills, while in the garden old cast iron cannons have been put to pasture.

Another interesting visit is to the exhibition of old whaling boats in a boathouse near the old port, open Monday to Friday 1400-1600.

Formalities

The Guarda Fiscal office is opposite the old fishing port, Porto da Calheta. An officer will probably meet the boat on arrival and carry out the formalities on the spot. The Capitania (Delegação Marítima) has an office in Rua Nova, which only needs to be visited by skippers of yachts clearing into the Azores for the first time.

Port Facilities

Mooring facilities in Santa Cruz are not good, so most visiting yachts stop at Praia, which offers better protection. In Santa Cruz one can come alongside the old quay, Cais do Freire, if there is no swell. There is at least 2 metres depth alongside this quay. The alternative is to anchor nearby. The bottom is mostly rocks and holding is not good, so one may wish to take one or two lines ashore provided they do not obstruct the few local boats which still use the port. The dinghy can be left at the steps on the main quay or at the steps by the ramp in the southwest corner of the port.

There is an old fashioned laundry house across the main road from the port, where one can do one's laundry. Otherwise there are no facilities close to the port, so it may be better to use the smaller anchorage in a well protected inlet close by the town centre. This narrow inlet has an old stone quay. It is possible to anchor in the inlet, which is perfectly protected in winds from south to northwest.

Marine Services

There are several small hardware stores in Santa Cruz but none of them stock any spares or equipment for boats. Gas (LPG) can be obtained from a small depot in Rua Serpa Pinto, past a furniture shop displaying the Tecnogas sign. Fuel is available from the GALP station in Largo Francisco Paulo Bettencourt, next to the police station, open Monday to Saturday 0800-2000, Sunday 0800-1400. There is a small quay behind the fuel station, where the dinghy could be conveniently left as it is close to the town centre. This is the alternative anchorage for Santa Cruz described above.

Hauling out

Boats can be hauled out only on the main quay at Praia with a crane belonging to the Port Authority.

Electrical repair

Alziro Soares, Rua da Olivença, Santa Cruz, Tel. 72371.

Diesel and outboard engines

Alziro Soares, see above.

Shore Facilities
Provisioning

The Supermercado Filnorte, Rua D. João IV, on the south side of the main square, open Monday to Friday 0900-2000, Saturday 0900-1700, is the best stocked in Santa Cruz. Another supermarket is on the opposite side of

Santa Cruz

INCORPORATED IN 1486

Santa Cruz, the attractive capital of Graciosa

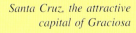
MUNICIPAL COUNCIL • Tel: 095 72124/72125

the square, Mercado Stop, Rua Serpa Pinto, open Monday to Friday 0830-1800, Saturday 0830-1300.

The bakery on Avenida Mouzinho de Albuquerque is difficult to find at the back of a small house next to the hospital. It is open Monday to Saturday 0800-1900 and has an excellent selection of local breads and also sells fresh meat.

Communications

The post office is in the same road, open Monday to Friday 0900-1230, 1400-1730, Tel. 72301, Fax 72141. Metered telephone calls can be made and faxes sent and received. There are also two public telephones in the main square, outside the Municipal Council.

Car Hire

Medina & Filhos, Rua Almeida Garret, Tel. 72278.

Medical

Hospital: Avenida Mouzinho de Albuquerque, Tel. 72110.

Tourist Information

Praça de Fontes Pereira de Melo, under the small bandstand in the centre of the main square, open Monday to Friday 0900-1230, 1330-1700.

CAIS DA BARRA

This well sheltered bay south of Santa Cruz is used by local sailors and is the site of the Graciosa Yacht Club. Most of the bay is taken up by local moorings, although there is space for anchoring in the southern part of the bay. There is 2 metres depth on the south side of the short quay, and steps on both its sides. There are two showers and a water tap on the south wall by the ramp, used mainly by people coming to swim. There is an old fashioned public laundry by the main road into Santa Cruz. There are no shops in the small village so for any shopping one has to walk one kilometre into Santa Cruz.

Yacht Club

The yacht club is in the process of acquiring a new building in Cais da Barra, which is supposed to be ready by the summer of 1994. Once it has its own

Cais da Barra

premises, the yacht club is keen to see more yachts visit Graciosa and will do its best to help those who are in need of local assistance.

Facilities

Although there are hardly any facilities in the small port, the situation may change once the yacht club has its new premises.

PRAIA

As its name indicates, Praia's main asset is its sandy beach and in summer it is popular with people from Santa Cruz who drive out for the afternoon. It is a small place with low one storey houses around the sea wall behind the beach. The road in and out of the town is lined with huge eucalyptus trees forming a canopy across the road and has a feeling of a tropical jungle about it.

The massive breakwater provides good protection from the prevailing northeast winds of summer, while the island itself gives shelter from the southwest, all of which makes Praia one of the best ports, not just on Graciosa, but anywhere in the Azores. As the port was built with commercial use in mind, amenities for pleasure craft are totally absent. A yacht may come alongside the main quay but one should clear this first with the Port Authority as boats on the quay are moved if a ship is expected. The best place to tie up is close to the root of the quay, where there is more space between the large tyre fenders.

A new red No. 2 buoy has been installed to mark the deeper channel

Praia

between the buoy and the green light on the end of the breakwater. Yachts are supposed to anchor well clear of this channel, preferably in the southern part of the harbour, south of a round red buoy, which has been laid by the port to mark the limit of the recommended anchorage. The centre of the harbour is taken up by private moorings. There is good anchoring in 5-6 metres on sand in front of the beach. The dinghy can be taken to the old quay at the entrance into the narrow fishing port. There is enough depth to come alongside this quay, either at its head or on its side, but the place is often occupied by local boats.

Although there is a small local fishing fleet, repair facilities are non-existent. In an emergency one should contact the Port Authority (Junta Autonoma), whose office is in the building by the old quay.

Formalities

The Guarda Fiscal office is on the waterfront in an older style building opposite the small fishing basin. An officer is on permanent duty and will clear in a yacht on arrival regardless of the time of day. However, if the yacht is at anchor, the skipper is not expected to go ashore immediately and if it is late can wait until the following morning. If one wishes to go into Santa Cruz, the Guarda Fiscal officer will call a taxi for the 6 km ride into town. The alternative is to call the car hire company who will deliver a car to Praia. The Capitania office is in Santa Cruz, but an officer comes to Praia every day, especially if a ship is expected. The Capitania need only be contacted by skippers of yachts clearing into the Azores for the first time.

Facilities

There are public showers on the waterfront, by the large arch leading to the beach.

The Minimarket in Rua Rodrigues Sampaio is near the church, open Monday to Saturday 0900-1700. This is the nearest shop to the port and has a reasonable selection of fresh fruit and vegetables. Bread is delivered daily from Santa Cruz and is best ordered in advance at the minimarket.

The post office is in Rua Barrão da Fonte do Mato, a road leading inland from the church, open daily 0930-1230.

The Shell station is next to the post office. It sells diesel and exchanges standard Portuguese gas bottles.

Toma-Lá-Dá-Cá is a small restaurant close to the port, overlooked by one of three windmills. It is open every day except Monday and serves lunches between 1200 and 1500 and dinners from 1800 to 2200. The food is good, simple and inexpensive.

CARAPACHO

Jagged rocks make this attractive stretch of the south coast rather treacherous, although in settled weather one could anchor right off the spa and then take the dinghy into the natural pool below the spa building.

FOLGA

A tiny fishing port with a short quay and ramp is in the bay below the village of the same name. The dinghy can be left at the concrete steps along the quay. There is sufficient depth to come alongside the quay, which in the past was used by the inter-island ferry, but as there is always some surge, anchoring is the better alternative. There are several moorings in the bay, but local fishermen haul their boats out as soon as they return from fishing. There is anchoring depth of 8 to 10 metres in the middle of the bay, which is sheltered from west through north to east.

A road leads into the village of Folga, 1/2 km inland. There is a water tap at the small restaurant at the top of the ramp. Restaurante da Folga is run by a local fisherman and his wife, the food is simple, as are the surroundings, but the fish is fresh. Meals should be ordered in advance. The only other building in the small port is a fisheries refrigeration plant, otherwise one has to walk into the village for provisions.

Folga

Porto Afonso

PORTO AFONSO

This deep bay in the lee of the point of the same name has a small quay and ramp which is used by a few fishermen who keep their gear in caves overlooking the small port. The bay is surrounded by high cliffs of volcanic rock in many hues making it an attractive day time stop in very settled weather. The bay is well protected in northerly winds.

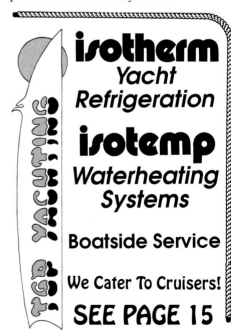

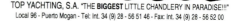

SÃO JORGE

Unlike other Azorean islands, São Jorge is long and narrow with a line of volcanic peaks running down its length, very often shrouded in a ribbon of cloud. Surrounded by steep cliffs, the island has a slightly forbidding appearance from the sea, which is deceptive as the central plateau is green and fertile. The island is neat and tidy with well tended terraced fields marching up the sides of hills to the rims of old craters. Most of the island is devoted to dairy farming and the distinctive São Jorge cheese is the best known and most widely sold of all the Azorean cheeses.

Although situated in the middle of the central group, São Jorge has in fact been one of the most isolated of the islands in days gone by. There is not a lot known about the early settlements, whose inhabitants appear to have come from Northern Portugal. A Flemish nobleman Wilhelm van der Haegen was among the first settlers and founded the village at Topo. He introduced the growing of woad and a lichen, which produces the purple dye orchil. Both of these dyes were exported to Flanders and other countries and played an important part in the early economy of the island.

For several centuries the island was isolated as it lacked sheltered ports and had little to trade. It also suffered several natural disasters, crop failure, food shortages, earthquakes and volcanic eruptions. The eruption of 1808 destroyed Urzelina and all that remains of the old village is the bell tower of the church sticking out of the lava.

The introduction of cattle raising and dairy farming, the building of an airport and ports at Velas and Calheta, have changed São Jorge's fortune and it now has an air of prosperity. This is especially noticeable in the many large new houses being built, mostly by returning emigrants from USA and Canada. Like from Horta, the view of neighbouring Pico from Velas can be superb and most houses are built to appreciate this view.

Steep cliffs surround almost all of São Jorge and reflecting this, great depths are carried close up to the shore. At various points in time the cliffs have slid down and formed low flat coastal areas which are called *fajã*. As the *fajã* often have fertile soil, villages grew up on and around these *fajã* and their fertile fields. Not all of them are accessible by road, some only by narrow paths zigzagging down the cliffs.

In several places waterfalls cascade down the cliffs adding to the majestic scenery. The cliffs tend to be very green, being clothed in the indigenous Azorean heather, which is bright green. Found throughout the Azores it is particularly abundant on São Jorge and in summer the central plateau is vividly coloured with huge banks of hydrangeas contrasting with the emerald green heather bushes and lush green fields dotted with black and white cows.

The beautiful vegetation of the Azores is seen at its best in the park at Sete Fontes, a reserve planted by the Forestry Commission near to Rosais at the western end of the island. Here flowers and bushes have been carefully landscaped to look wild and a myriad birds sing in the protected area. Nearby is a viewpoint, from where one can look down on Velas and across to Pico, Faial and Graciosa.

As one climbs up the central ridge towards the highest point Pico da Esperança at over 1000 metres, the vegetation changes, there are no trees or hydrangeas, but grass carpeted with yellow flowers. On a clear day one can see all the islands in the central group.

The eastern end of the island towards

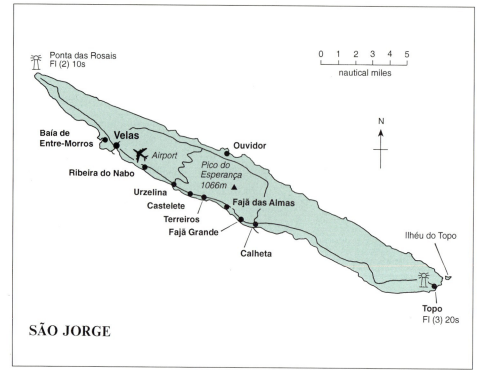

Topo is more remote and has an older, more leisured atmosphere with farmers going to their fields on horseback or driving magnificent oxen pulling wooden carts filled with hay.

NAVIGATION

The more sheltered south coast has several attractive anchorages where one can spend the day and the two ports of Velas and Calheta are situated on this coast. Between Velas and Calheta is the small port of Urzelina which is the second largest settlement on the island. From Urzelina eastward, the coast has dramatic black volcanic formations with arches and grottoes, the rocks looking almost as if they have been sculpted. One large cavern is easily accessible by dinghy from the anchorage at Urzelina, but the whole area can be enjoyed by sailing close along it.

Sailing eastward one passes several *fajã*, the villages nestling at the foot of towering cliffs. The scenery between Fajã das Almas and Calheta becomes even more dramatic with vertical cliffs topped by the cones of extinct volcanoes on the skyline high above. There is deep water right up to the shore and one can sail along almost touching the sides of the cliffs. The cliffs become lower as one approaches Calheta, the small port serving the eastern end of the island. From here to Topo, at the eastern extremity of the island, the coast is mostly inaccessible, with the few villages built inland. There are a few day anchorages, such as at Portal and Fajã de São João, but there are no natural harbours or protected bays along this entire stretch of coast. It is dramatic scenery to be enjoyed in passing.

Off the eastern extremity of the island lies the small islet of Topo, which is a nature reserve and one of the nesting sites in the Azores of the roseate terns, which are a threatened species. It is an offence to enter the nesting colonies and boats are requested to keep at least 50 metres away.

São Jorge's north coast is wild and

CÂMARA MUNICIPAL DAS VELAS
SÃO JORGE - AZORES

WELCOME TO VELAS

Velas Town and Harbour

View of Pico from Velas

Urzelina

Ouvidor

Tel: 095 42214/42882 – Fax: 095 42351

rocky with steep cliffs. With the exception of Ouvidor, there are no anchorages along its entire length. At the western extremity off Ponta Rosais is another rocky islet, nesting site for sea birds.

LIGHTS

Rosais   38°45'.23N 28°18'.79W
Fl(2) W 10s 260m 8M
Velas   38°40'.7N 28°12'.3W
Fl R 5s 7m 7M
Ponta da Queimada 38°40'N 28°11'.6W
Fl W 5s 50m 12M
Urzelina   38°38'.6N 28°07'.7W
Fl R 6s 10m 6M
Calheta   38°36'.1N 28°00'.6W
Oc R 3s 18m 7M
Ribeira Seca   38°35'.7N 27°58'.9W
Fl W 3s 72m 10M
Ponta do Topo   38°33'.0N 27°45'.3W
Fl(3) W 20s 58m 20M
Norte Grande   38°40'.8N 28°03'.1W
Fl W 6s 12M

PONTA ROSAIS

This is an attractive day anchorage right under the lighthouse which is perched above. The anchorage is overlooked by huge vertical cliffs. One can anchor close in to the rocky beach and there is good diving on nearby rocks.

BAÍA DE ENTRE-MORROS

Only one mile west of Velas, this is one of the few natural bays on the island, protected from the east and southeast by the Morro Grande headland, and from the west by the equally high Morro de Lemos headland. The secluded anchorage provides good shelter from most directions except the southwest, but because of the unreliable holding ground, it should only be used as a day anchorage. There is 5 metre anchoring depth at the head of the bay, very close to the rocky beach. The water appears discoloured in some places, but this is due to whitish boulders with some sandy patches in between. Everywhere in the bay, the bottom is large boulders with poor holding, unless the anchor fouls in one of the gullies. A batch of lobster pots in the east of the bay should be avoided.

VELAS

The main town of Vila das Velas has many attractive old buildings fronted by a substantial harbour wall designed to rebuff piratical attack. The town is built on a *fajã* and the port has a beautiful setting being surrounded by high cliffs. The many birds nesting in these cliffs attract one's attention as night falls by their distinctive call, sounding like chattering gossips. On the town side, the old fortifying wall runs around the port and a large 18th century gateway leads from the quay to the town beyond. The town itself is very quiet after bustling Ponta Delgada or Horta, the pace being more tranquil, as it is on the whole island. The black and white parish church of São Jorge fronts a large square from where buses run to the rest of the island. In the centre of town, a smaller square is alive with flowers and shrubs, providing an oasis for the townspeople to sit and pass the time of day. By the botanical garden high above the town is a small house where one can see local weaving being done on large wooden looms, making the patchwork counterpanes for which São Jorge is renowned.

Outside the ramparts surrounding the harbour is a natural swimming pool created among a group of rocks, which has a paved area around it and a café on a terrace with a view across to Pico.

There are several days of festivities during the town's main feast, held every year during the weekend following 8 July, Portuguese Navy Day. Artists come from continental Portugal and Brazil as well as from neighbouring islands. A yacht race from Horta was started in 1983 to coincide with this fiesta and now the race is established, it brings some 30 or 40 yachts, both local and visiting cruising boats, to join in the festivities.

Formalities

The Guarda Fiscal is on the corner of the nearest building to the main quay.

The office is open 24 hours a day and should be visited as soon as possible after arrival. It is also required that skippers call at the Capitania office, which is also located on the waterfront at the opposite end of the block to the Guarda Fiscal building. The Capitania is open Monday to Friday 0900-1230, 1400-1730.

Port Facilities

The main quay has been extended recently, which has increased the protection inside this harbour. An inner quay was also added and is used mainly by the inter-island ferry. Yachts may come alongside the main quay if there is space, but it is usually taken up by small fishing boats, often rafted up. Large tyres are used as fenders, so smaller boats are better off if they can come alongside between two tyres. Metal ladders lead down to water level making it easier to climb up the high wall. There are some concrete steps either side of the large container crane.

The smaller inner quay is used by the inter-island ferry and one should only come alongside if the ferry is not expected and one is prepared to moved out at very short notice. There is 3 metre depth along the quay with a set of concrete steps halfway along.

Most of the anchoring space inside the harbour is taken up by moorings laid down by local fishermen. The moorings which were laid down a few years ago for the use of visiting yachts have mostly disappeared and as it is impossible to ascertain which of the remaining ones could hold a yacht, it is better to use one's own anchor which can be dropped east or southeast of the local moorings. The water is clear, but the holding ground is rather unreliable, rocks with patches of sand. The dinghy is best left at one of the steps described above. As the harbour is open to the southeast and a sea breeze often springs up from that direction on summer afternoons, the anchor should be checked if leaving the boat unattended for any length of time.

Velas

Facilities in the port itself are very basic and the nearest water tap is in the Guarda Fiscal building. With permission one can take water from there and carry it in jerrycans to the boat.

Marine Services

Although there is a sizeable local fishing fleet, the range of facilities is limited. Most workshops are on Avenida do Livramento, on the outskirts of Velas.

Chandlery

A new chandlery, as yet without a name, was opened in the summer of 1993 in Rua das Caravelas 15, which overlooks the port. Although the selection available is quite basic, the young owner will order items from Ponta Delgada.

Diesel Engines

José Almeida, Avenida do Livramento, Tel. 42301, is the best diesel mechanic used by the local fishing fleet.

Juliano Moura, Avenida do Livramento, Tel. 42292. This is another workshop used by the local fishing boats.

Outboard Engines

Manuel Soares, Rua de Pos 16, a small workshop overlooking the inner quay.

Electronics Repair

Eduardo Maciel, Avenida do Livramento, Tel. 42479.

Carlos Azevedo, Avenida do Livramento, Tel. 86419.

Woodwork

There is a carpenter at Largo Dr João Pereira 13.

Fuel

The GALP station is in Largo Dr João Pereira, in front of the parish church, open Monday to Saturday 0800-1900, Sunday 0800-1300. Large quantities of fuel are delivered in drums to the main quay, smaller quantities must be carried in jerrycans.

Shore Facilities

There are some public showers in the café overlooking the swimming area behind the ramparts. These are within walking distance of the port.

Provisioning

Supermercado Soares, in Largo das Almas, is open Monday to Friday 0830-1900, Saturday 0830-1500. A good selection of staple goods, fresh fruit, vegetables and local cheeses.

Loja Espírito Santo, on the corner of Largo Dr João Pereira, is the nearest supermarket to the port, but does not have such a wide selection of goods.

Loja Matriz, on the corner of Rua da Matriz, near the parish church. Open Monday to Saturday 0800-2000, Sunday 0800-1200. Although small, it has a good selection.

The bakery, Padaria de Velas, Rua de São José, is open Monday to Saturday 0700-1300, 1400-1600.

Communications

The post office is in Rua Dr. Miguel Teineira, open Monday to Friday 0900-1230, 1400-1800. Metered telephone calls can be made and faxes sent and received (Fax 42676). There is a cardphone near the GALP fuel station in the square by the parish church.

Laundry

Residencial Neto, a guest house in Rua Dr José Pereira, the street leading up from the port, will take in laundry and charge the same rates as for their own guests.

Car Hire

J.N.Moura, Av. do Livramento, Tel. 42292.

Almeida Azevedo, Tel. 42410.

Medical

Health Centre: Rua Corpo Santo, Tel. 42122.

Restaurants

Velense, Rua Dr José Pereira. As it is almost the only restaurant in town it is often very busy and serves both lunches and dinners.

Tourist Information

Rua Dr José Pereira, Tel.42440, open Monday to Friday 0900-1230, 1400-1730.

RIBEIRA DO NABO

This day anchorage one mile west of Urzelina has an old stone pier and steps

Urzelina

leading down to the water. There are a few new buildings ashore but no village to speak of.

URZELINA

The second largest settlement on the island stretches westwards from the small port. Two distinctive windmills stand on the western headland. There is an attractive village nearby used mostly as a holiday resort. On the west side of the bay water is piped up from the sea to a large seawater swimming pool and in summer there is a campsite behind the pool. The village has been completely rebuilt since being destroyed by a volcanic eruption in 1808. All that survived is the bell tower, incongruously standing out of the lava which buried the old church. Now in a garden reached through a small gate, one can climb up the tower. An old fortress with cannons in its ramparts guards the centre of the bay, but it is now a bar and night club. There are several bars in the village, including the Castelinho restaurant, which overlooks the port.

The Centro de Exposição Rural, in the small square by the quay, has an interesting exhibition of farming tools, wine presses and old furniture.

The anchorage off the village is in a small, but well protected, rocky bay with an old quay on its western side. There is a light ashore and by entering on a bearing of 35°M all dangers are avoided. There is a large rock in the southeast part of harbour which should be avoided when anchoring. There is no space on the small quay to take even the smallest yacht. There are several moorings used by local boats, which are hauled onto the ramp if there is too much swell. The best anchorage is in 10 metres in the middle on the bay. The dinghy can be taken either to the old quay on the west side, or near the ramp where there is another set of steps on the northeast side by the derrick.

There is a water tap across from the swimming pool. The Supermercado A Torre, by the old church tower, open daily 0800-2000 has fresh and frozen goods as well as bread. It is run by a young couple who have returned from California, speak good English and are keen to be of help to visitors.

CASTELETE

A small bay with a stony beach overlooked by a cluster of houses. There is a small quay and steps near a crane and ramp.

TERREIROS

This small inlet has its own stone pier and a few houses nearby, while the rest of the village, overlooked by a large church, is to the northeast. There is a group of rocks and shallows in the southwest part of the bay, which should be entered on a northerly heading to avoid all dangers.

FAJÃ DAS ALMAS

This open bay with a small village on the rocky promontory is overlooked by steep cliffs covered in evergreen heather. There are a few fishing boats on moorings and the usual stone pier and ramp, where the dinghy can be taken. A very steep road winds up to the main road.

FAJÃ GRANDE

This is not much more than a group of jagged rocks in attractive surroundings. A ramp and steps lead down to the water where the dinghy can be landed. There is 12 metres depth some 100 metres south of the rocks where one can anchor in settled weather. The anchorage is overlooked by a restaurant, which in turn is overlooked by a red windmill, one of many which have been restored along this stretch of coast.

CALHETA

The village of whitewashed houses is strung out along the road climbing the slope out of town. Although it has only a population of 350, this is swelled during the music festival Calheta hosts every July, when singers and groups are invited both from mainland Portugal and other islands. A stage is set up on the town quay and the street is lively with booths and foodstalls.

There are two rocks about a quarter of a mile west of the harbour entrance, so one should not follow the shore line too closely before turning into the small port. There is sufficient depth alongside most of the main quay facing northeast, but this should only be used if the inter-island ferry is not expected. The quay is rather high and as there are no steps or ladders access can be very difficult at low water. Shallow drafted boats may prefer to come alongside on the northwest side of the quay as it turns in towards the ramp, but there is only 1.5 metres depth there. There are some moorings on the east side of the bay and one should anchor clear of these. The dinghy is best left at a set of concrete steps by the crane on the inner quay mentioned above.

The Guarda Fiscal is in a white building close to the ramp, open Monday to Friday 0900-1230, 1400-1730, Saturday 0900-1230. An officer is on permanent duty, although the office is only open at the above hours.

Facilities

Although Calheta has a small fishing fleet, repair facilities are almost nonexistent. There is a good mechanic called Luis in Ribeira Seca, the next village to the east, and he can be contacted via the chief of the Guarda Fiscal in Calheta.

There is a water tap on the west side of the quay where the local fishing boats

Calheta

are hauled out. Fuel can be obtained from the GALP station, on the northwest corner of the large square by the quay.

Antigua Rua da Praça leads west out of the square, with various shops, the Municipal Council, and post office along it. The post office is open Monday to Friday 0900-1230, 1400-1800. Metered telephone calls can be made from the counter. There is also a public telephone outside the Municipal Council building.

There is a small grocery on the waterfront, opposite the Guarda Fiscal office, selling mainly local vegetables and some fruit. Supermercado Jacil, Rua Azevedo da Cunha, is on the way to Fajã Grande, approximately 1 km west from the port. Open Monday to Friday 0900-1300, 1400-1800, Saturday 0900-1300. It has a good selection, including fresh fruit, vegetables, meat and an excellent cheese counter. The bakery, Padaria Calheta, is next to Supermercado Jacil.

The tourist information office is next to the Municipal Council, open Monday to Friday 0900-1230, 1400-1730, and every day during the Calheta Music Festival in July.

TOPO

Once an important port used by the ferry from Terceira, this remote harbour at the eastern extremity of São Jorge is now used only occasionally by the inter-island ferry. The harbour offers protection in winds from southwest through west to northeast, but some swell makes itself felt even in calm

Topo

Ouvidor

weather. There is a quay on the northern side with 4 metres depth alongside it and a set of concrete steps by the crane. There is a water tap in the building above the quay. A steep ramp leads to the road going to the village of Topo about 1 km away where one can find the usual selection of small shops. The post office is on the way out of the village, on the road to Calheta.

OUVIDOR

This is the only anchorage on São Jorge's north coast. The bay is very well protected in winds from east through south to west. Although providing perfect shelter in winds from those directions, the anchorage should be left quickly if the winds changes to the north. There are anchoring depths anywhere in the bay. The few scattered shallower spots are easily seen in good light. There is a small quay and steps on the north side but there is not sufficient depth to take a yacht alongside.

There is a water tap, toilets and outside shower in a white building on the ramp. A steep walk leads into the village which is clustered on the hillside overlooking the bay. There is a small shop near the crossroads as well as O Alberto's bar and restaurant which overlooks the port and affords an excellent view of the beautiful bay towards Canada da Anegadas, a circle of rocks on the eastern side of the bay. Alberto is a rubicund local whose appearance is the best advertisement for the cooking of his wife, mainly fish dishes, which have to be ordered in advance.

PICO

Pico, the most distinctive of all the Azorean islands, takes its name from the volcanic peak, which rises 2351 metres (7700 feet) above the sea and dominates not only its own island but all those that surround it. Its perfect splendour is not always visible, often the upper portion hides behind clouds and the whole island can be invisible from Faial only five miles away. Dramatically, sometimes only the peak is visible, while the lower island remains shrouded in mist. Often it tantalises, the summit slipping out of the cloud for a few minutes then disappearing back into its wreath. In winter snow blankets the summit, while when Pico wears a hat of cloud, a change in weather is reputed to be on its way.

On a clear day the view from the top is magnificent, with Faial, São Jorge, Graciosa and Terceira visible. It is not an easy climb as the road only goes part of the way. Enthusiastic travellers plan to spend the night at the top to catch both sunset and sunrise.

Apart from the volcano itself, nature has endowed Pico with many other interesting features. Close to the edge of Pico's crater is a secondary cone, or Little Pico, where fumaroles still remind one that the volcano is only sleeping and that at some point in the next 10,000 years it will blow its top. On the plateau are several small lakes surrounded by forest. Scores of smaller cones and craters, evidence of past volcanic activity are also scattered on the plateau. In several places are black lava fields called 'mysteries' as their formation in the 16th and 18th centuries was regarded as mysterious by the inhabitants. The escaping of gases and the cooling of lava have produced vast caverns and long galleries going deep into the hillside, dangerous to visit without a local guide. More accessible is Arcos do Cachorro on the north coast, a dramatic place where black volcanic rocks are twisted into weird shapes with rocks arching over the sea, which surges into caverns and grottoes.

The rich volcanic soil has produced a very distinctive wine, which was exported all over the world until hit by blight in the 19th century. The vines were replanted, but Pico wine never regained its previous renown. The wine should perhaps be sampled with the cheese for which the island is also famous. Often called 'the orchard of the Azores', fruit of all kinds is grown, both temperate and tropical, figs and plums being particularly well known for their quality.

The southern shores of Pico are calmer and more sheltered with land terraced right up to the volcano, the black dry stone walls bounding the tiny fields green with vines, bananas, maize and potatoes. In contrast, the north side of the island is more forested and the road lined with hydrangeas and wild roses mixed with small white daisies. Orange nasturtiums and purple convolvulus make equally dramatic hedgerows. The black volcanic rock has been used extensively in building, the houses typically having black dressed stone outlining windows and doors in contrast to the whitewashed walls. Echoing the same theme, black and white churches with twin towers are the focus point of each village.

The history of Pico has always been tied up with Faial and Madalena developed as the principal town mainly due to its sea links with Horta. The first settlement on the island was at Lajes, which was the principal town and port for many years and the whaling capital of the Azores.

American whalers first came to hunt in the area in the 18th century and gradually they recruited men from the islands as harpooners and rowers. The pool of skilled fishermen in the islands formed the basis of the emigration of

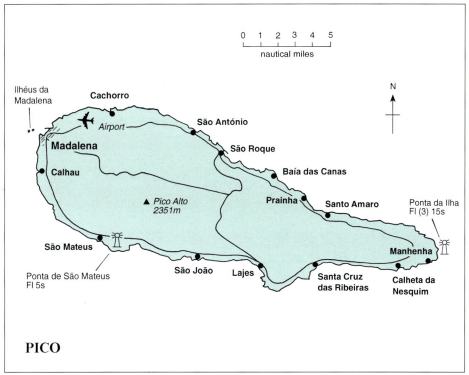

PICO

Azoreans and their families to whaling centres abroad, notably in New Bedford in the USA, but also as far afield as California and Hawaii. Later in the 19th century the men of Pico started hunting for whales themselves in small open boats. The Azoreans hunted whales in this traditional way from open boats until fairly recently. In the heyday of the industry some 300 whales a year were processed in the large factory at São Roque on the north coast. In Lajes there is an interesting whaling museum which has a good collection of scrimshaw. This art is still alive in Pico, home of the best scrimshanders in the Azores and their scrimshaw can be bought in Lajes.

NAVIGATION

Because the prevailing winds in summer are from the north or northeast, the south coast of Pico is mostly in the lee and all ports and bays are protected from those directions. There is always some residual swell and a slight surge makes itself felt in all ports, but apart from the inevitable rolling of the boat, there is little else to worry about.

Leaving Madalena to sail anticlockwise around Pico, the two rocky islets, Ilheus da Madalena, should be left to port. Although there is depth in the channel between the islets and the coast, it should only be used with local knowledge. Attention should also be paid to the tides in the channel separating Pico from Faial, which sometimes set strongly causing some overfalls and steep seas when the wind is blowing against the tide.

There are more ports and anchorages on Pico than on almost any of the other islands and on a cruise along the south coast, Lajes do Pico, Santa Cruz das Ribeiras and Calheta de Nesquim are all worth a visit.

The eastern end of the island is marked by the light at Ponta da Ilha and the village of Manhenha stands southwest of the lighthouse. The protection offered from the north and

Madalena

northeast by the island of São Jorge makes the north coast of Pico accessible in winds from those directions, provided they are not too strong. There are several anchorages that can be used in calm or light conditions, while the best protected port is at São Roque. Going west from Cachorro to Madalena, the rocky coast is black, forbidding and sombre. Even the houses in the few hamlets have a forbidding look, having been built out of blocks of lava, the black mortarless stone walls giving the abandoned villages a sombre look.

LIGHTS
Madalena   38°32'.2N 28°32'.0W
Oc R 3s 12m 10M
Areia Larga   38°31'.6N 28°32'.2W
Iso R 4s 11m 7M
Calhau   38°29'.2N 28°32'.4W
Oc R 3s 11m 6M
São Mateus   38°25'.4N 28°27'.0W
Fl W 5s 34m 13M
Lajes do Pico   38°23'.9N 28°15'.4W
Fl G 5s 7m 3M
Santa Cruz das Ribeiras   38°24'.4N 28°11'.2W   Fl R 3s 14m 14M
Calheta de Nesquim   38°24'.2N 28°04'.7W   Fl R 5s 14m 7M
Manhenha   38°24'.6N 28°02'.2W
Fl R 5s 13m 6M
Ponta da Ilha   38°24'.8N 28°01'.9W
Fl(3) W 15s 29m 24M
Santo Amaro   38°27'.4N 28°10'.1W
Oc R 6s 7m 7M
Prainha   38°28'.5N 28°12'.1W
Fl R 4s 15m 7M
São Roque   38°31'.9N 28°19'.2W
Fl G 3s 10m 2M

MADALENA

The principal town of Pico started off as a small fishing port of some charm and has grown rapidly in recent years, its prominence due primariily to the frequent ferry service from Horta. This role was even more important before Pico built its own airport, but even now jet airplanes can only land on Faial, so visitors to Pico have to transfer to a smaller plane or make the crossing in the fast ferry. In fact many visiting sailors prefer to come to Pico by ferry, leaving their yachts in Horta Marina.

The church of Santa Maria Madalena, with its elegant black and white facade, dominates the waterfront and is particularly attractive from the anchorage when it is decorated with lights for a feast day. The main festivities are associated with the day of the patron saint of the city, Mary Magdalen, and celebrations are spread over several days. On the afternoon of 23 July the statue of Mary Magdalen is taken out of the church and carried in procession through the streets. An even more interesting procession takes place on Espírito Santo day when scores of baskets piled high with a special bread are displayed in front of the church and later processed through the streets.

Another local curiosity, until recently only known to a few people, is Joao Queresma's whisky collection. In his younger days, Sr Queresma was a shipping agent who rather than drink the bottles of whisky given to him by the captains of visiting ships, collected them in his home. Now in his eighties, Sr Queresma has gathered a unique collection of well over one thousand different brands, not just Scotch, Irish, bourbon or rye, but also whiskies from distilleries in the Far East and other, less traditional origins. Arrangements to visit Sr Queresma's collection, which is in the main square by the church, should be made through the Municipal Council.

Approaches

Two distinctive rocky islets, called Ilhéu Deitado (lying down) and Ilhéu Em Pé (standing) are home to nesting seabirds. They guard the harbour entrance and mark the approach to Madalena. One should leave these islets to starboard on entering the port and not attempt to go between them and the island.

Formalities

The Guarda Fiscal is in Rua Carlos Dabney, around the corner from the Town Hall (Câmara Municipal). The office is open Monday to Friday 0900-1230, 1400-1730. Yachts arriving outside of those hours are usually visited

WELCOME TO MADALENA

Contact: Municipal Council, Tel: 092-622280 Fax: 092-622722

by a Guarda Fiscal officer, and also by an official from the Capitania. The latter's office, Posto Maritimo, is next to the post office, in the square outside the main church, and is open daily 0800-2130. The officer is always in the port to meet every ferry and he usually calls at the same time on yachts which have recently arrived.

Port Facilities

For those who wish to come alongside one of the quays, there is always space somewhere. The main northwest quay is used by a fleet of tuna fishing boats and there is always much movement along this quay. It can also be noisy as the boats leave their generators running. The thrice daily ferry from Horta uses the northeast side of the shorter inner quay. There is space to come alongside the southwest side of this ferry quay. There are no amenities for visiting yachts in the port apart from toilets in the ferry terminal. There is water on the dock, but arrangements must be made to have it turned on.

There are seven moorings southeast of the ferry dock and four more moorings in the southern part of the harbour. The former are closer to the steps, but also noisier, being closer to all the activity. The latter are quieter and better protected from all directions, except west, although it is a longer row ashore. The moorings have been laid down for the use of visiting yachts by the Junta Autonoma de Porto da Horta and are marked with the initials JAPH. The inlet where the four moorings are offers even some protection from the southwest, a direction to which the rest of the harbour is open. From the southern mooring area, the dinghy can be taken to a set of steps and metal ladder set in a quay used by local swimmers, but it is not wise to leave it there when this is crowded with children diving in the water. There is a water tap in the road overlooking the swimming area. A cobbled street leads into town past the building of the local yacht club.

Yacht Club

Clube Naval de Madalena, Esplanada de Clube Naval, is located on the small esplanade south of the town. The club offices are on the first floor in an older building on whose ground floor is a snack bar. Visiting sailors are welcome to use the bar and should approach the club for any practical help.

Marine Services

Boatyard

As the base of a large ocean going tuna fishing fleet, Madalena has the benefit of better than average repair facilities. Most of these are in the hands of COMPICO, the shipyard based in the port of Madalena. The yard has several slipways, both for larger and smaller vessels. The yard can handle any kind of work on diesel engines, welding, hydraulics, fibreglass and wood. It can also undertake electrical repairs on alternators or generators. COMPICO, Madalena, Tel. 623 002.

Chandlery

Manuel Dutra de Feria, Rua Dr Freitas Pimentel, Tel. 622 455, open Monday to Friday 0800-1200, 1400-1800, Saturday 0800-1200. A limited range of nautical equipment, marine paints, cordage, filters and general hardware.

Electronic repair

Electro Radar, Rua Dr Freitas Pimentel, Tel. 622 215, open Monday to Friday 0800-1200, 1400-1800, Saturday 0800-1200. The shop is located immediately past the fish market, on the road going south from the main square. The owner, Manuel Gonçalves dos Santos, is a skilled electronics engineer, who is used to dealing with the demands of a large fishing fleet and has repaired a variety of radars, radios, depth sounders, etc. He speaks good Spanish, English and French.

Fuel

There is no fuel in the port and the only fuel station is a Mobil station, on Rua Carlos Dabney 56, Tel. 622 416, about one km out of town on the road to the airport.

Shore Facilities

Provisioning

Supermercado Heltina, Rua Maria de Gloria Duarte, Tel. 622 490, open Monday to Friday 0700-1930, Saturday 0700-1230. Located in a small street on the left as one walks from the port into town, it has a good selection of food as well as fresh fruit and vegetables.

Supermercado Olimar, Rua Eng. Alvaro Freitas, Tel. 622 362 open every day including public holidays, 0800-2300. This has a poorer selection than the other supermarket, but longer opening hours.

There is no municipal market but local farmers usually sell their produce in the street by the main church. There is a fish market, open Monday to Saturdays in the mornings, in a small street south of the main church.

Padaria Andrade in Avenida Machado Serpa has the reputation of baking some of the best bread in the Azores. It is worth asking for their *pão caseiro*, a wholemeal bread, or *pão saloio*, rye bread, but even their ordinary rolls are excellent. They also make cakes and pastries. Open Monday to Saturday 0700-1600.

Restaurant

Golfinho, Rua Carlos Dabney, is a small but good restaurant serving fish and other dishes.

Communications

The post office is in the square by the church, open Monday to Friday 0900-1230, 1400-1800. Metered calls can be made and faxes sent and received (Fax 622 202, Tel. 622 201). There are two public telephones in Largo Jaime Ferreira.

Car hire

Colombis Rent-a-Car, Avenida Machado Serpa, Tel. 622 601. They also have an office in the ferry terminal.

Medical

Hospital: Praça Dr Caetano Mendoza Tel. 622 241.

PORTO CALHAU

This small port on Pico's southwestern coast is used by a few fishermen from the nearby village of Monte. The small bay is overlooked by O Calhau, the best fish restaurant on the island, Tel. 622 757. An old breakwater gives some protection from the south and east. There is anchoring depth west of the breakwater and the dinghy can be taken to the steps near the head of the quay. There is always some surge which is the reason why local boats are craned onto the quay when they return from fishing.

PORTO SÃO MATEUS

The small cove open to the south has a short breakwater and slip on its western side. A dozen fishing boats are usually pulled up on the ramp, as is normal along this coast. There are no shops anywhere near the small port, although a snack bar will be opened shortly in a house overlooking the port next to a small chapel built in 1753.

RENT A CAR

QUALITY SERVICE

Av. Machado Serpa
9950 MADALENA
Tel/Fax: 62 26 01

Lajes do Pico

Shops and a bank are in the large village of São Mateus about 1 km inland. Along the road leading up to the village are two ancient dragon trees with the names of local fishermen carved into their branches.

PORTO SÃO JOÃO

There are several bays east of the light on Ponta de São Mateus which may be used as day anchorages. In a small bay below the village of São João is a small port with a breakwater to protect it from the southwest. There is a group of rocks southwest of the breakwater but they are all above water and clearly visible. There is at least 2 metres depth to come alongside the short wharf, but there is always some surge. Otherwise one can anchor close to the quay and take the dinghy to the steps. There is a water tap on the quay. A small seafood restaurant (Marisqueria) overlooks the port, so one does not have to walk far to sample some of the local specialities. It is a steep walk into the village which has several small shops and cafés.

LAJES DO PICO

The oldest town on the island has lost its importance because of the demise of the whaling industry, but also due to the lack of a safe port. The town is rather attractive, with many old houses in the typical Pico style with black dressed stones along the seafront. The Chapel of São Pedro is the oldest church on the island, being built in 1460, while the Franciscan convent attached to the main church is now the Town Hall. The former boathouse on the main quay has been made into a Whaling Museum, reflecting the days when Lajes was the whale hunting centre for the region. The museum houses a traditional whaling boat and other artifacts and includes a big collection of scrimshaw. One can also watch a video of one of the last times a whale was hunted from an open rowing boat in the traditional Azorean fashion.

Approaches

The bay is encumbered with rocks, only some of which are visible at low tide. The entrance into the perfectly protected harbour should not be attempted without local advice or at least a prior visit by dinghy to identify the deeper entrance channel. The latter is marked by leading beacons (one with a green top on the end of the breakwater and two with red top markers on the hill behind the town). The channel avoids the rocks and has at least 1.50 m at high water. The problem is that at low water, there may not be sufficient depth alongside the quay, so even if one has a boat that does not draw much, it may be better to stay outside at anchor. There is a relatively good spot some 300 metres to the west of the end of the breakwater but the holding ground is not too good and should not be relied upon. Everywhere there are deep gullies and large boulders, which can foul one's anchor, so a trip line is strongly advised.

Formalities

The Posto Maritimo (Capitania) is close to the port, next to the Moby Dick cafeteria. Lajes is not a port of entry and boats arriving from overseas must call at one of the official ports of entry first. If coming from another island in the Azores, the Capitania should be visited first and they will advise if one should also go to the Guarda Fiscal office.

Facilities

Facilities in the port itself are limited. Yachts normally anchor as close to the end of the quay as safety permits and then take the dinghy to the set of steps at the western end of the quay, which is used by swimmers. As fuel is not available in the port, this would have to be carried in jerrycans from the fuel station, located in the main square. Next to it is a taxi rank and also a coin operated public telephone. Opposite the church is the post and telephone office, open 0900 - 1230, 1400 - 1800 Monday to Friday. Metered telephone calls can be made and also faxes sent and received at this office (Fax 97328). In the same street there is a small supermarket as well as a butcher selling fresh meat and some local fruit and vegetables. In typical Azorean fashion, none of these shops has a sign outside. This description also fits the fairly well stocked hardware store, near the main square, which also exchanges gas bottles, the latter being clearly displayed on the pavement.

Whaling Museum (Museu dos Baleeiros), open 0930-1230, 1400-1700, Tuesday to Saturday, only afternoons 1400-1700 Sundays and holidays, closed on Mondays.

SANTA CRUZ DAS RIBEIRAS

This pleasant little port should not be missed. The approaches are quite clear, but if coming from the west, the breakwater is obscured by the rocky foreshore and only becomes obvious when one is almost next to it. Usually there is space along the quay and as local fishing boats prefer to go nearer the western, shallower end, visitors are less likely to be moved if they come alongside the end of the breakwater, where the depth is 4 metres at low water. There is always some surge.

There is an interesting Mariners Home in the boathouse facing the slipway, where in the old whaling days the whales used to be hauled out. Two original whaling boats have been nostalgically preserved inside, both fully equipped with spars, sails, long oars and lethal harpoons. The old men who use the place as a club explained that the last whale was hunted over ten years ago and stressed that Azoreans hunted whales by traditional means, their boats being driven by wind and oars, while only hand thrown harpoons were used. At least the whales had a fair chance.

There are two groceries in the village, one near the church, with a limited selection, and a surprisingly well stocked supermarket in the main street. The latter sells fresh rolls daily, some fresh locally grown fruit and vegetables, as

Santa Cruz das Ribeiras

well as the delightful local cheese produced by a dairy outside the village. There is a coin operated telephone behind the Mariners Home.

CALHETA DE NESQUIM

This small village has a tiny harbour tucked in behind a solid breakwater, a leftover from the days when this was a major whaling port. An impressive church in the typical Pico style overlooks and dominates the picturesque port, where all the harbour walls of black rock are carefully outlined in white. Outside the church is a small square with old balconied houses and the ubiquitous bandstand. The village clustered around the church and port is deceptively small, as most of its houses are fanned out on the surrounding hills which climb up in neat terraced fields right up to the crater overlooking the village.

In settled weather keeled boats can enter the small harbour, but attention should be paid to a group of rocks close to southeast. There is a deep channel between the rocks and the end of the breakwater. Two red leading lights lead past all dangers. A 30 degree turn to port should be made after the end of the breakwater has been passed. There is a 4 m depth on the outer part of the quay, diminishing to 3 metres where the quay curves towards the ramp. Occasionally the space on the quay is taken up by a larger fishing boat, but there is always some space to come alongside as the local fishing fleet is very small and the boats are usually pulled up on the ramp. The port is well protected and there is little or no swell inside.

Café Beira Mar stands at the top of the ramp leading into the village. There is a minimarket in the square below the church and also a water tap by the steps leading up to the church.

MANHENHA

The village of Manhenha stands southwest of the lighthouse at Ponta da Ilha on the eastern end of the island, from which it is separated by a number of small bays. There is a ramp and steps in front of the village. Overlooking the small inlet is a snack bar belonging to Liga dos Amigos de Manhenha, where old men gather for a chat in the afternoons.

Calheta da Nesquim

Santo Amaro

SANTO AMARO

This small port on the north coast is the home of one of the biggest shipbuilders in the archipelago, the locally based Marmar company being the builder of most offshore tuna fishing boats operating out of the Azores. The boats are built in wood by traditional methods, the local shipwrights using mostly hand tools.

Leading lights lead into the small port which is open to northeast. The short quay is usually taken up by local boats. There is 4 metre depth on the outer quay, decreasing to 2.5 metres inside the small pool. If there is not too much surge, one should attempt to come alongside the main east facing quay. Otherwise one can anchor in the bay and take the dinghy to one of several sets of steps. There are no facilities in the port, although water was being laid on in the summer of 1993.

The village of Santo Amaro spreads out on both sides of the port. A well stocked minimarket is about 100 metres on the road going west from the port. There is a small boatyard along this road and there is no doubt that help would be forthcoming from either yard in an emergency.

PRAINHA

A large church dominates this small town which is one of the oldest settlements on the island. One of the main reasons for its decline is the absence of a good harbour. There is now only an old quay east of the lighthouse and the place is mostly deserted outside of the holiday season.

BAIA DAS CANAS

A black sandy beach, inaccessible from the land, makes a good day anchorage when the winds are in the south.

SÃO ROQUE

Also referred to as Cais do Pico, on account of its quay (*cais*), the correct name is that of the neighbouring town of São Roque. It was the site of the only whaling factory in the islands. São Roque is an old town with interesting houses and mosaic pavements all along its long seafront. Next to the baroque church of São Pedro is a former Franciscan monastery, now housing the police station, in front of which are some unusual mushroom shaped trees and a towering Norfolk pine.

As São Roque is closer to the road leading up towards the summit of Pico, and also the safest port on the island, this might be a better base than Madalena from which to make the necessary arrangements to climb to the top of the mountain.

A massive breakwater with a large quay for container ships provides the best protected port on the island. Along most of the quay are large tyres used as fenders. Small boats should therefore use the western end of the quay, near its root, where there are no large fenders and a couple of local boats are usually tied up.

A yacht may fare better to come alongside the old quay in front of the deserted whaling factory. There is 3 metres depth at the head of the quay and 2 metres on the inside (south side), by the steps, but this place is used by a local excursion boat. The north side of the quay has sufficient depth for only a few metres of its length. Further in there are large boulders in the water making it dangerous for a keeled boat.

São Roque

Formalities

Boats are usually met by a Guarda Fiscal official on arrival. Otherwise the skipper should walk into town to complete formalities. Both offices to be visited are on the waterfront, the Delagação Maritima (Capitania) is close to the post office in a white one story building with radio masts on its roof. The Guarda Fiscal building has a red steepled roof and is opposite the small boat ramp. The Port Authority office is in a low building inside the container park.

Facilities

The local yacht club, Clube Naval São Roque de Pico, opposite the old quay, has a small snack bar, which is open every day in summer from 0900-2100. Visiting sailors are welcome to use the few existing facilities. In the rear of the building is a workshop for the maintenance of a small fleet of sailing dinghies, where it would be possible to make small repairs. Club members can advise visitors where larger repairs could be done.

There are showers and a water tap on the south side of the ramp. There is no fuel in the port and only one Shell station in town, in Rua Coronel Linhares de Lima. On the corner of the same street and the avenue fronting the sea is the post office, open Monday to Friday 0900-1230, 1400-1800. There are booths for metered calls and faxes can also be sent and received there (Fax 642 102). There are a couple of small supermarkets, the Minimercado Soares, Rua Coronel Linhares de Lima, next to the Shell station and further east along the waterfront, Loja de Jaiminho, which is a larger supermarket with a better selection of fresh fruit and vegetables, fresh bread, local wines and also some hardware. There is a taxi rank on the waterfront, or taxis can be ordered by telephone on 642 125, 642 497.

SÃO ANTONIO

There is a deep inlet here among huge volcanic rocks. The dinghy can be taken either up the narrow ramp or to the metal ladder close to the swimming pool. Worth visiting is the old church built in 1696 in the small village spreading to the west of the small port.

CACHORRO

Nowhere is the coast more striking than at Arcos de Cachorro, where jumbled rocks, twisted arches and deep inlets with water boiling over submerged ledges show nature at its wildest.

There is a relatively well protected bay on the west side. One can anchor in the bay west southwest of the small stone wharf, but only in settled weather. Concrete steps lead up to a platform where a couple of small fishing boats are hauled up with the help of a derrick.

FAIAL

The island of Faial and the port of Horta hold a special place in the affection of all the sailors who call there for this small island has a long involvement with the sea, ships and those who sail in them. The first yachtsman who recorded his stay there was Joshua Slocum on *Spray* and like many a sailor after him, he tarried longer than he had planned.

I remained four days at Faial, and that was two days more than I had intended to stay. It was the kindness of the islanders.... which detained me.

During the 1920's and 1930's the number of yachts calling was two or three a year, then this doubled and from the 1950's onward the trickle became a flood with now nearly one thousand yachts calling every year. The majority of these, in May and June, are Europebound after crossing the Atlantic and few of them visit any other islands besides Faial. Many sailors do not even venture outside the town of Horta, which dominates the history and culture of the island. This is a pity because there is much to see outside of the town.

In the centre of the island is a volcanic cone with a vast dramatic caldera 400 metres (1300 feet) deep, with luxuriantly wooded slopes in varying shades of green. From the rim on a clear day one can see over the whole island and across to Pico, São Jorge and occasionally Graciosa.

Faial has been the victim of several volcanic eruptions, but none greater than from September 1957 to October 1958. Starting with 200 small earthquakes in the space of ten days, there was then a submarine eruption off the western point of the island close to Capelinhos. This eruption continued in violence with jets of steam raining ash and pumice over the western end of the island. An island 100 metres high was formed which eventually joined to Faial to form a new headland. This activity continued off and on with flows of lava until it finally ceased in October 1958. In all over 300 houses were destroyed.

Although a new headland was born, this has been partly eroded by the sea, while vegetation is creeping back across the ashy wastes. This part of Faial is eerie to visit with ruined houses covered in ash and the old lighthouse forlornly isolated amidst a lunar landscape instead of standing proudly on a headland. A small museum in the next village documents the eruption. Vulcanologists continuously monitor the earth tremors, which have become particularly frequent recently, although most are too faint to be felt.

In contrast to the bare Capelinhos area, where yellow lilies and succulents contrast with the black sand, the rest of the island is lush, the hedgerows full of colourful flowers, pink roses, red cannas, orange nasturtiums and purple convolvulus. The green fields are bordered by hedgerows of hydrangeas, which in June and July are in full bloom, which has given it the name of Blue Island (*Ilha Azul*).

Some people imagine that the name Horta comes from *Hydrangea hortensia*, but this is not a native plant and the name of the town derives from Josse van Huerte, a leading Flemish settler in the early years of the town's history.

The island of Faial prospered peacefully until 1583 when the Spanish attacked and waged a battle at the gates of the Santa Cruz fortress, which overlooks the marina. During sixty years of Spanish rule, the town was also sacked by English privateers, in 1589 by the Earl of Cumberland and in 1597 by Sir Walter Raleigh, who burnt Horta to the ground. Returned to Portuguese rule, the following centuries were fairly peaceful and the island prospered.

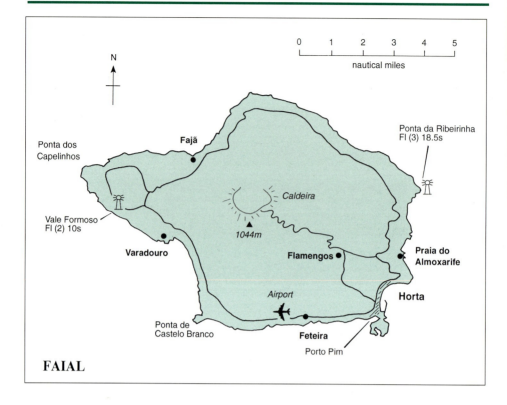

FAIAL

NAVIGATION

Horta's excellent marina precludes most people from visiting the rest of Faial by boat and they circumnavigate the island either by taxi or hired car. This is undoubtedly the most comfortable way of seeing more of this beautiful island, where nature appears to have spent all its energy inland to the detriment of any natural harbours. The few bays are only suitable in settled weather and even then should only be considered as day stops.

LIGHTS

Horta Breakwater 38°32'.0N 28°37'.3W
Fl R 3s 21m 11M
Ribeirinha 38°35'.8N 28°36'.2W
FL(3) W 18.5s 47m 28M
Vale Formoso 38°34'.9N 28°48'.7W
Fl(2) W 10s 114m 13M
Feiteira 38°31'.0N 28°41'.0W
Oc G 6s 9m 5M

HORTA

The town of Horta dominates Faial and the history of the island is very much the history of Horta. Most of its prominence has been due to the development of the port. At the beginning of the 19th century a farsighted American, John Dabney, arrived and started the warehouses which attracted ships to Horta for provisioning and repair. The Dabney family were involved in exporting Pico wine and oranges until blights devastated both crops, but it was due to their activity that the port of Horta developed. In the 19th century, the rich whale hunting in the region brought the whaling fleets to Horta in increasing numbers and the bay has had as many as 400 vessels at anchor there at one time. The whalers came to provision, rest, offload whale oil and also to recruit crew, the Azorean sailors having a good reputation. Many Azoreans

JUNTA AUTÓNOMA DO PORTO DA HORTA

Av. Gago Coutinho e Sacadura Cabral, 7 • 9990 HORTA
Tel: 092 - 221164/5/6
Fax: 092 - 22523

HORTA MARINA

Cais Velho • 9990 HORTA

Faial • Azores • Tel: 092 - 31693

sailing with the fleets eventually settled in New Bedford in the USA, which is twin city to Horta.

In 1876 work started on the breakwater to give better protection to the port and this attracted steamships to fuel as well as the traditional sailing vessels. A new phase in the story of Horta began with the laying of a submarine cable from Horta to Lisbon and this was followed by cables in all direction, including across the Atlantic. British, Italian, French, German and American companies made their base on Faial. At the same time Horta became one of the most important telegraphic centres of that era, particularly for communicating meteorological observations for forecasting purposes, giving the rest of the world a chance to know the position of that all important Azores high.

The importance of knowing the details of the Azores weather in forecasting was appreciated by Prince Albert of Monaco, who led several oceanographic expeditions to the islands in his yacht *Hirondelle* and was instrumental in the building of the meteorological observatory on the hill overlooking Horta that is now called the Prince Albert Observatory.

The importance of the telegraph cable is reflected in the Horta newspaper *O Telégrafo*, founded in 1893 and which is still published today, recording the names of all yachts calling.

The large cable industry resulted in many fine buildings being built in Horta, both as offices and as quarters for the expatriate staff. The lively social scene and cosmopolitan atmosphere only ended in 1969 when the last cable company departed leaving the satellites to do their work instead.

Some of Horta's most interesting moments were to do with early air travel. In 1919 Albert Read landed with his fragile seaplane making the first transatlantic crossing of the Atlantic. Many others followed, pilots of all nationalities in all kinds of flying machines choosing Horta as a stop in their transatlantic flight. In 1933 Lindbergh flew in to assess the feasibility of Horta as a stopover and soon afterwards the giant Pan American clipper seaplanes started regular flights between Europe and America via Horta. Lufthansa, Air France and Imperial Airways, the predecessor of British Airways, all established bases in Horta in the later 1930's, but the days of the flying boat were numbered as the superiority of land based planes increased and another era in Horta's history passed by. The Atlantic weather also proved a disadvantage and seaplanes could not always land and take off. This resulted in the passengers of one Pan Am clipper flight being stranded in Horta for several weeks. They relieved their boredom by publishing a newspaper called *The Swell* and copies of this can be seen in the office of the local airline SATA in Horta. Now it is the turn of the yachts, whose importance in the island economy was recognised by the opening of a new yacht marina in 1986 in the centre of town under the old fort of Santa Cruz.

The town of Horta runs around the bay and across the narrow isthmus to the bay of Porto Pim. There are many fine houses with different coloured facades, verandas and curious shaped garrets in the eaves from where ships or whales could be spotted. The town has several fine old churches in typical Azorean style. Gracious mansions were built by the Dabney family and many fine buildings by the cable companies, which now have been put to other uses such as a hotel or offices. An impressive example of 1930's architecture is the large Amor da Pátria club. Horta is one of the administrative centres of the Azores and the Ministry of Tourism and Environment is based in the town.

For a magnificent view of the town one can climb up Monte da Guia, which rises behind the port and is separated

Horta

ESTALAGEM DE SANTA CRUZ

Set in historic surroundings in a medieval fortress, the Estalagem of Santa Cruz overlooks the marina and waterfront in the heart of Horta.

25 twin rooms, 18 with a sea view, each with a private bathroom, telephone, colour tv and radio.

Restaurant with seating for 80 persons, bar, lounge, games room and conference room for 60 persons. Chapel for weddings and christenings.

Rua Vasco da Gama, 9900 HORTA Tel: 092 - 23021/23022

from Horta by a narrow isthmus. There is a small chapel here and one can look down on all sides, over the port of Horta, Porto Pim and the Caldeira do Inferno.

Nautical Icons

The marina has become a tourist attraction in itself, due mainly to the brightly coloured paintings on the walls done by visiting sailors. From early cave painting to modern graffiti, man seems to fulfil a primeval urge in leaving his mark for posterity, a permanent record for all to see that he passed that way. Nowhere is this popular art form more alive than in the port of Horta.

No one is quite sure who it was or when it was, that a sailor first took up paints and brushes to adorn the seawall of this harbour with a pictorial record of his boat and ocean passage. Over the years the huge wall filled up with paintings, images of all the long distance sailors who had passed through the Azores. As time went by sailors were forced into gymnastic feats to find a free space. By the time the new marina was opened in 1986 the old wall was completely covered.

The artistic talent latent in the sailing community is quite considerable and with a tempting virgin wall surrounding the new marina, the wall paintings of Horta reached new artistic heights. Now the new marina walls are virtually full, and it is taking increasing ingenuity to find a space and the paintings have overflown onto the quay and docksides.

Sailors are notoriously superstitious and legend has it that is unlucky to set sail without recording your name on the Horta wall. Local sailors quote several examples of boats that got into trouble after leaving without making their painted offering to the gods. Everyone arriving here has come from far afield and leaves with far to go, so that the gods of the fabled Atlantis cannot be ignored.

Game Fishing

The Azores and Horta particularly is gaining an international reputation as an excellent place for game fishing. A number of sport fishing boats have made their base in Horta attracting sport fishermen from all over the world. They fish mainly for blue and white marlin, swordfish and shark. Several European records are broken every season and they have also established a number of world records, such as a 274 kg (604 lb) blue marlin landed on a 12 lb line as well as a 524kg (1156 lbs) marlin caught on a 50 lb line by the yacht *Double Header*, while the yacht *Shanghai* established a European record with a 477 kg (1051 lb) blue marlin caught on a 80 lb line. In order to preserve stocks, the captains of the boats make a point of not landing a fish unless they are sure that it is a world or European record, in which case they have to be taken ashore to be weighed and assessed. Otherwise all fish are released.

Café Sport

Few sailors pass Horta by without making their way to the blue fronted Café Sport overlooking the harbour. Once listed by *Newsweek* as one of the world's best bars, Café Sport has featured in many articles and television programmes. Its fame is due to the Azevedo family who have been welcoming sailors to Horta's shores for many years. According to family lore, this began with the welcome given to Joshua Slocum by the grandfather of the present owner Peter Azevedo. It was Peter's father Henrique who built up the tradition of welcoming sailors to his bar, a tradition that Peter turned into an institution and is now carried on by his son José. Pennants and burgees decorate the ceiling and walls, interspersed with T-shirts and gifts from grateful yachtsmen.

In 1966 Peter started his first guest book and now has over sixty. The early books read like a history of yachting, with Erick Tabarly and his first *Pen Duick* close to Humphrey Barton on *Rose Rambler* and Eric and Susan Hiscock on *Wanderer III*. Francis Chichester and *Gipsy Moth* only made it into the second book. Peter Azevedo's other passion over the years has been collecting old scrimshaw and his museum above the café displays his fine collection of beautifully etched whales' teeth, as well as his most cherished yachting mementos. Café Sport is moving to larger premises and it will be interesting to see if the same atmosphere prevails in the new café.

Not such a well known face to visitors is Joao Carlos Fraga, who has perhaps done more than anyone else to put Horta on the yachting scene. Yachting adviser to the Azores government, he has a finger in many pies, but always in the interest of the sailor. Always to be found on the dock when an interesting vessel appears, he is still there to help when another has a problem. It is the people who make Horta what is, not the buildings in it, a charming town with a welcoming face to the stranger.

Approaches

On arrival in the harbour boats should tie up at the reception dock, in front of the marina office, where there is 4 metres depth. During peak arrival time, between May and July, it is usually necessary to raft up several boats deep. There is less than 1 metre depth on the south side of the reception dock and 2 metres on the north side, so keeled yachts are better docked along the east facing quay.

Entry Formalities

Entry formalities should be completed while on the reception dock. The marina office should be visited first, open daily in summer 0800-1200, 1300-2000. In winter the office closes at 1700 and on Sunday afternoons. Next the skipper should visit the neighbouring Capitania, whose office has the same office hours as the marina during summer. The office is closed in winter, but an officer will come to the marina when called by the marina staff.

The next office to be visited is the Guarda Fiscal, also on the reception dock and having the same hours as the marina. A Guarda Fiscal officer is always

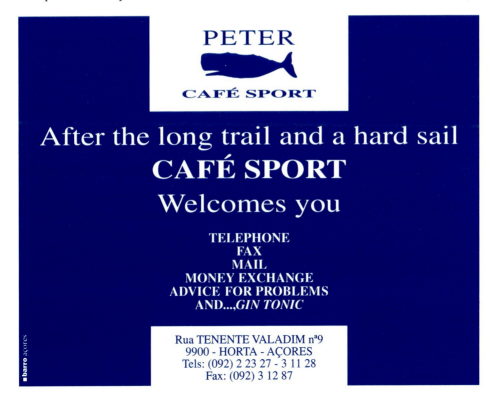

on duty in the marina, but will only clear in boats during office hours.

Horta Marina

The marina monitors VHF Channel 16 during normal working hours. The two marina staff, Luis Morais and José Lobão, speak both English and French. Berths are only allocated after entry formalities have been completed, so every yacht must stop first at the reception dock. It is advisable to fill up with fuel on arrival so boats do not have to stop on departure when the dock may be full with boats waiting to be cleared.

The marina has some 200 berths on three floating pontoons, individual berths having their own finger pontoons. There is water and electricity at every slip. Smaller boats, up to 11 metres LOA, are normally berthed on the floating pontoons. As there are no dead moorings, boats should come alongside the finger pontoon and keep themselves away from the main pontoon with spring lines. Larger yachts and multihulls are berthed alongside the outer wall, where depending on numbers boats are rafted up two or three deep. If there is space, larger boats are assigned a space at the end of one of the floating pontoons. Occasionally, larger yachts may be allowed to spend one or two days on the reception dock but as this interferes with the fuel dock, boats are moved away as soon as possible. On the rare occasions when the marina is completely full, large yachts may be berthed alongside the main quay in the commercial harbour. There are plans to extend the reception dock in a southerly direction and create additional docking space in that area.

Marina fees are reasonable and in 1993, boats between 10 and 12 metres paid 1060 escudos per day, plus 12% VAT, while those between 12 and 15 metres paid 1325 escudos plus tax. Water and electricity are included in these fees. Boats which are left for longer periods, especially during winter, are given a large discount if fees are paid in advance. The marina accepts payment by Visa credit card.

Port Facilities

A utilities block in the northern part of the marina, containing showers and laundry, is open daily from 0800-1145, 1300-1900. A charge of 200 escudos per person is made for the use of a shower, for which a large towel and soap are provided. Washing machine and driers are also available in the same block, the cost for one load, washed and dried, including detergent, being 1000 escudos. The charge for washing only is 500 escudos. There is also a bar serving light snacks.

There is a card phone at the shower block, while metered calls can be made from the marina office. Faxes can be sent and received through the marina (Fax 22523). The charge per page sent is 1700 escudos, which is the same as the charge made at the post office. There is no charge for incoming faxes. The marina can also be used for holding mail. Mail should be addressed to the yacht, c/o Horta Marina, Cais Velho, 9900 Horta, Azores, Portugal. Tel. 31693, Fax 22523.

Weather

A daily prognosis is posted on the window outside the marina office and also on the bulletin board outside the Capitania office, south of the marina. Horta has its own meteorological institute, the Meteorological Observatory Prince Albert of Monaco, from where one may request a long term forecast. This is best done through the marina office.

Yacht Club

Clube Naval da Horta, Cais Velho, Tel. & Fax 22331, is the most active yacht club in the Azores. Now located in a modernistic building south of the marina, the club is open to visitors who are welcome to use its bar and also join one of its many races. First visitors should visit the club secretariat, which is open Monday to Friday 0900-1230, 1400-1830. The office is also open at weekends during the racing season and monitors VHF channels 16 and 72. The bar is open daily from 1200(noon)-0200.

The racing season is from May to September and every event attracts a large number of visiting yachts. Although local sailors take racing quite seriously, the rules are not always strictly enforced and handicapping visiting yachts is often a joke. However, the partying before and after each race more than makes up for any frustration one might feel at being denied a prize because of a result based on "incorrected" time. The most important races in the annual calendar are:

Autonomous Region Cup: held on Espírito Santo Day (May or June)

Round Faial Race: 10 June

Atlantis Cup (Horta-Angra do Heroísmo-Ponta Delgada): end of June. An excellent way of seeing the Azores is to join this event which goes to the three main islands: Faial, Terceira and São Miguel.

Horta-Velas-Horta: a two day event held during the weekend closest to 8 July, Portuguese Navy Day. The sponsor in São Jorge, where Saturday night is spent, is the Municipal Council of Velas, which pulls out all stops to welcome the 30 or more yachts which usually join this event.

Sea Week: held between the first and second Sundays in August, with yacht races on Monday, Wednesday, Friday and Sunday, a most successful series of races around buoys in the straits between Faial and Pico. Singlehanded and lady skipper races are also on the programme as well as various dinghy races. The annual Sea Week, which started in 1975, attracts spectators and participants from all over the Azores, as well as mainland Portugal, for a weeklong series of shows, sporting events, civic functions and nightly concerts in the park overlooking Horta Marina.

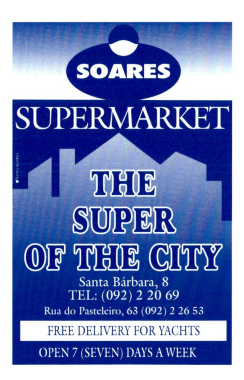

SOARES
SUPERMARKET
THE SUPER OF THE CITY
Santa Bárbara, 8
TEL: (092) 2 20 69
Rua do Pasteleiro, 63 (092) 2 26 53
FREE DELIVERY FOR YACHTS
OPEN 7 (SEVEN) DAYS A WEEK

YACHTING CENTRE OF THE ATLANTIC
SAILING
CANOEING
ROWING
FISHING
DIVING
PAVILHÃO NÁUTICO
9900 HORTA
FAIAL, AÇORES
Tel: (092) 22331
Fax: (092) 22331
CLUBE NAVAL DA HORTA

FAIAL

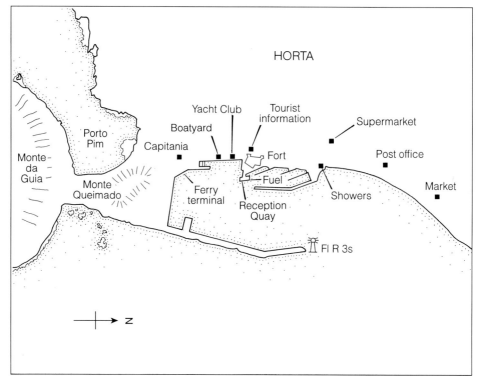

Marine Services

Boatyard

A self-service yard operates on the quay south of the marina. Boats are hauled out by arrangements with the Horta Port Authority (Junta Autonoma do Porto da Horta), which has a number of cranes. There is a 40 ton crane on the main quay in the commercial harbour, for which the hourly charge is 20,000 escudos. The hourly charges for the mobile cranes are: 17,500 escudos for the 40 ton crane, 12,500 escudos for the 30 ton crane and 7,500 escudos for the 20 ton crane. Owners usually do their own work as there is no established boatyard. If any specialist work is needed, arrangements have to be made with the relevant individuals.

Chandleries

Náutica Horta, Rua Visconde Leite Perry 2, Tel. 23757. Located in the square near the municipal market this small chandlery is operated by the man who runs the Mobil station in the marina. The shop has a reasonable selection of yachting hardware, fishing gear and a good range of International paints. Whatever is not available can be ordered from Lisbon. As agents for Perkins engines, they also hold a selection of fuel and oil filters and other consumables. Open Monday to Friday 0900-1300, 1400-1800, Saturday 0900-1300.

Bazar Rosa, Rua Conselheiro Medeiros 24, Tel 23171. Located close to the marina, this older chandlery has a smaller selection. Open Monday to Friday 0900-1300, 1400-1800, Saturday 0900-1300.

Hardware

There are several hardware stores on the main street, some also selling a limited selection of boating equipment.

Teófilo Ferreira Garcia, Rua Vasco da Gama 18, a well stocked hardware store close to the marina.

CIN, a paint shop at the beginning of the main street, has a good selection of paints and is the nearest to the marina to buy the paints for the work of art every passing boat is expected to leave behind. By tradition, the rest of the paint is passed on to the next artist.

Charts
Policia Maritima, next to Capitania da Horta, has an office selling Portuguese charts, both of the Azores and mainland Portugal. The cost is 2600 escudos per chart. The office is open Monday to Friday 0900-1200, 1400-1700.

Mid-Atlantic Yacht Services, Rua Conselheiro Miguel da Silveira, Tel. 31616, have a small selection of cruising guides.

Electrical Repair
Manuel Antonio da Rosa, Bairro Mouzinho de Albuquerque. A skilled electrician for alternator and generator repairs. Contact via marina office.

Electronic Repair
Náutica Horta, see above, agents for Autohelm, Koden, Shipmate, Sailor. Will not repair locally but send equipment for repair to Lisbon. No duty will have to be paid on parts imported to replace items under guarantee.

Borba & Soares, Rua Angústias 70, Tel. 23656. The company also operates under the name Electro Radio Maritima. Mario Soares speaks good English and has been recommended as a skilled and reliable engineer.

Refrigeration Repair
Manuel Antonio da Rosa, contact via marina office.

Diesel Engines
Náutica Horta, see above, agents for Perkins, Mitsubishi, Solé.

Manuel Gomes, a skilled engineer working for the Port Authority can be contacted via the marina office.

Matiflago Lda, Rua Serpa Pinto 25, Tel. 23283.

Outboard Engines
Náutica Horta, see above, Honda and Yamaha agents. .

Fibreglass Repair
Delfim Vargas, Tel. 22218, for small repairs.

Fibromar, Santo Amaro, Pico, Tel. 655132. A boatbuilder on the

EVERY DAY IS SPRING AT PRIMAVERA

Open in the lunch-hour

Light snacks and refreshments available

Free delivery to yachts in Horta Marina

Video Club

SUPERMERCADO PRIMAVERA
Tv. S. Francisco - 9900 HORTA
Tel: 22116/7 - Fax: 22617

RENT A CAR

ILHAZUL

RUA CONSELHEIRO MEDEIROS, 14
TEL: 092-31150/22969
FAX: 092-31360
TELEX: 82576 MARSIL - P
9900 HORTA
HOURS: DAILY 0800 - 2200

neighbouring island of Pico skilled in fibreglass construction and repair.

Sail Repair

Ralf Holzerland, Tel. 23149. A German recently settled in Faial, Ralf has been commended by several people whose sails he has repaired. He also does canvas work, awnings and tents.

Woodwork

Carpintaria Silva, São João 43, Tel. 22168.

Metalwork

Manuel Gomes, contact through marina office.

Fuel

Diesel is available from the Mobil station on the reception dock, open daily 0800-1200, 1300-2000 (summer). In winter only until 1700. Although the marina will accept credit card payments for berthing, only cash payments are accepted for fuel.

Petrol (gasoline) can be bought from the fuel station in Rua Vasco da Gama, next to the yacht club.

Gas Filling

Bensaúde & Co., Rua Tenente Valadin, next to Café Sport, for butane and Camping Gaz.

Mid-Atlantic Yacht Services, see above.

Diving

The yacht club (Clube Naval) has a compressor and will fill tanks for non-members.

Shore Facilities

Provisioning

Supermercado Primavera, Rua São Francisco, Tel. 22116, off Horta's main street, open 0830-1900 Monday to Friday, 0830-1300 Saturdays, has a good selection of tinned food as well as fresh produce including local cheeses. Free delivery to marina.

Supermercado Soares, 2 km out of Horta on the road to Flamengos, open Monday to Saturday 0900-2000, Sunday 1000-1800, Tel. 22069. A new supermarket with the best selection on the island, competitively priced goods, and a good place to reprovision for a long passage. They will deliver to the marina and will also send a car to collect those without transportation.

Costa & Martins, Rua Conselheiro Medeiros, Tel. 22141, open Monday to Friday 0900-1200, 1300-1700, Saturday 0900-1300. A wholesaler also selling retail, close to the marina, has a good selection of wines and spirits, some tinned food, as well as engine oils.

The bakery is on Rua Walter Bensaúde 17, open Monday to Friday 0700 - 1800, Saturday 0700 -1300.

The municipal market is open Monday to Friday 0700-1500, Saturday 0700-1300. Locally grown fruit and vegetables, also fresh meat and eggs.

Laundry

Horta Marina has several washing machines as well as one dryer, but these cannot be used on a self-service basis. A marina employee will load the machines. The charge is 500 escudos for one load, including detergent. An additional charge of 500 escudos is made for the use of the dryer.

Lavandaria Rosa, Rua Fernando da Costa, Tel. 31557, open daily 0900-2100. The service of this laundry may be more convenient as they collect and deliver to and from marina if telephoned.

Communications

The Post Office, Largo Duque d'Avila e Bolama, is open Monday to Friday 0830 - 1830. Metered telephone calls can be made from the office, and faxes sent and received (Fax 22170). There are also public telephones, both coin and card operated, outside the post office for use outside hours. Metered calls can also be made and faxes sent from Horta Marina office. Both Café Sport and Mid-Atlantic Services offer similar metered telephone calls.

Café Sport, Rua Tenente Valadim, Tel: 22327 Fax. 31287.

Café Sport is much more than a bar, it provides many essential services besides watering the wandering sailor, mailing address, long distance telephone calls and money exchange at any hour.

Mid-Atlantic Services, Rua Conselheiro Miguel da Silveira, Tel. 31616. They offer mail holding, fax and telephone service, book and magazine exchange. They also act as middlemen for repairs or chandlery orders for which they charge a commission. Located close to the marina, the small office is open Monday to Friday 0900-1300, 1400-1800, Saturday 0900-1400. Metered telephone calls can be made and received from their two booths and faxes can also be sent or received (Fax 31656). They also will look after yachts left in the marina during winter, making regular checks against chafe, bilge pumps, etc.

Car Hire

IlhAzul, Rua Conselheiro Medeiros 14, Tel. 22950 & 33150.

Autoturística Faialense, Rua Conselheiro Medeiros 12, Tel. 22308, 23608 & 99203.

Bike Rental

Protur, Rua Tenente Valadim, next to Café Sport, Tel. 22146, open Monday to Friday 0900-1300, 1400-1700, Saturday 0900-1300. On Sundays, it is open between 0900 and 1200 in Rua Ilha Ventura 8c. Bicycles and scooters for rent.

Restaurants

Canto da Doca, Rua Nova, although officially called Dock's Corner due to its location near the commercial port, everyone refers to it as Helder's Pub. Its owner, Helder Castro, is a typical Azorean gone to America to seek his fortune, but returned from California still young and full of energy. In a place where it is impossible to have dinner after 10 pm. he will serve dinner until 2 or 3am if there is a demand. This is possible as the clients cook the fish, prawns or steak themselves on special granite stones heated to 400°C.

Estalagem, Santa Cruz fort, this small hotel overlooking the marina also has a restaurant open to the public having an excellent menu and wine list. The place to go in Horta for a special occasion.

Medical

Hospital: Rua Principe Alberto de Monaco, Tel. 22122.

CALDEIRA DO INFERNO

A perfectly protected bay on the south side of Mount Guia whose ominous sounding name (Hell's Crater) conceals one of the most beautiful anchorages in the Azores. Because the perfectly shaped submerged crater has been declared a nature reserve and access by power boats is prohibited, those who wish to visit and anchor should try to do so under sail. Permission to visit must be obtained from the Capitania.

PORTO PIM

This shallow bay south of Horta offers excellent protection from any direction except southwest. As it is so close to Horta Marina, from which it is only separated by a narrow neck of land, this natural harbour is seldom visited by yachts, although during settled summer weather it provides an attractive alternative to the marina itself.

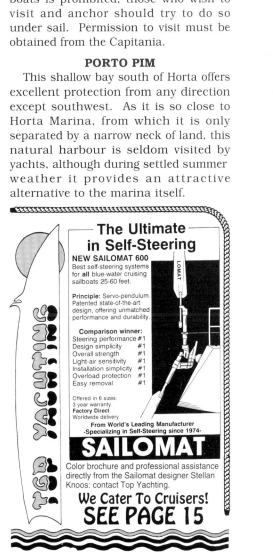

FETEIRA

Some of the best diving is close to this village where two rocky inlets, at Punta Furada, are separated by a lava arch which has been scooped out of the black cliffs by the sea. There is anchoring depth close to either inlet, which abound in underwater grottoes, but there is always some swell.

VARADOURO

A holiday resort whose popularity is mainly due to the tidal pools that exist among the volcanic rocks. Steps lead up to a public shower block. The other attraction of this summer resort is the Vista da Baia restaurant, run by Frank and Mary Vargas, an American couple of Portuguese extraction whose speciality is barbecued chicken basted in a deliciously spicy sauce. The best anchorage is close to the restaurant in 8 to 10 metres off a small inlet. The dinghy can be taken to a set of steps on the west side of the inlet.

The view from the restaurant is that of Castelo Branco, which marks Faial's southwestern extremity. The wide bay between Varadouro and the headland is overlooked by steep cliffs, but is without any special attraction except to those who are interested in diving as both close to the north of Castelo Branco and along Faial's south coast diving and underwater fishing are excellent.

CAPELINHO

Those who prefer to visit the site of the last volcanic eruption by boat, rather than overland as most people seem to do, have the choice of two anchorages, both of which are relatively safe during settled northeasterly winds. In any other kind of weather they should only be considered as day anchorages. Both anchorages are close to the old Capelinho lighthouse, which was destroyed during the eruption of 1957. The more northerly of the two anchorages is in the lee of the newly formed headland. There are several submerged rocks to the south, but there are no dangers if the anchorage is entered from the northwest. A large rock is clearly visible above water due west of the rocky beach. As the area has not been charted, and the land is still being eroded and continually changing shape, it should be approached carefully and only in good light.

The other anchorage is southwest of the old lighthouse and is protected by a line of rocks, which have also created a small pool. The dinghy can be left at the concrete slipway which is used by local fishermen to launch their boats, a few of which are pulled up on the rocky shore.

FAJÃ

This small bay has a black sandy beach near a small village consisting mostly of holiday homes. The anchorage is relatively safe and free of swell but only during northeasterly winds. There is a public toilet and shower in a nearby parking lot by the beach. A steep 2 km walk leads to the larger settlement of Praia do Norte, which has a few shops, café and public telephone.

PRAIA DO ALMOXARIFE

This anchorage is only one and a half miles to the north of Horta, immediately beyond Ponta de Espalamanca, which protects Horta harbour from that direction. Behind the black sandy beach is a small square with three restaurants, one of them having a small minimarket. There is also a public telephone in the square, but not much else as the place is mostly used by people from Horta who come on a day's outing to the beach.

Capelinho

CORVO

Corvo is the smallest and most isolated of the Azores and until very recently was the only island without a passenger airport. A boat runs from Flores once or twice a week, weather permitting, to supply the population of 350 souls.

Discovered at the same time as Flores around 1450, it was only settled in the next century. Today, as they did in those days, the islanders live by farming and fishing in a self-reliant community.

There has never been a military garrison on Corvo and in spite of the islanders' heroic stand against a fleet of Barbary ships in 1632, throughout most of their history the locals seem to have reached a rather useful relationship with the marauding pirates and privateers. Of course they always pretended to be the King's loyal subjects, but it was an open secret that the islanders made a good living out of supplying the pirates' basic needs. With no land to the west for at least 1000 miles, the latter were quite dependent on the goodwill of the islanders. This may account for their special character and independence of spirit which is acknowledged even by the other Azoreans. The isolation of the island has meant that many archaic words have been preserved in the islanders' language.

When in need of a doctor or priest, the islanders used to signal by bonfire to Flores, but the telephone makes emergencies easier to deal with today, especially as the island can be cut off for days by the typical haze which can render both islands invisible one from another.

The coastline is quite rocky with several islets and rocks of interesting shapes, including one like a statue, which faces west and is reputed to be that of a knight pointing the way to America. In spite of its small size, Corvo still boasts an extinct volcano, Monte Gordo, which has a large crater, some 300 metres deep and over 3 kilometres around. There are two lakes at the bottom of the crater with a couple of small islets.

Only in settled weather can a yacht anchor off the only settlement on the island at Vila Nova, which is the smallest town borough in Portugal.

LIGHTS

Ponta Negra   39°40'.1N   31°06'.6W
Fl W 5s 23m 6M
Canto da Carneira 39°43'N   31°05'.1W
Fl W 6s 238m 9M

VILA NOVA

Narrow streets paved with pebbles and black stone houses edged in white characterise this small town. Some of the houses have doors with curious locks with wooden keys. However, in such a small community houses are rarely locked and some do not have any locks at all. The interior of the village church, Nossa Senhora dos Milagros is striking in its simplicity. The name of the island patron betrays the miracles performed by the Madonna in 1632 when the islanders were besieged by an overwhelming force of pirate ships. The Flemish carving of the Madonna which adorns the altar is taken in procession through the streets on 15 August.

The narrow Rua da Matriz leads past the church into a small square where old men sit on stone benches chatting the time away. According to Dr João Cardigos dos Reis, president of the Municipal Council, the only way to capture the essence of the island is to spend at least one night ashore. If one walks through the quiet streets in the early hours, one may notice that some people are not asleep, but sitting outside their doors quietly chatting to their neighbours.

Dr Cardigos dos Reis had been practising medicine on the island for ten years before he decided that he could serve the small community better as the island's president. During his term he has done much to improve the lot of his constituents, but he may not stand for re-election in 1994 as he intends to return to his medical practice. However, he will continue to be available for advice or help to visiting sailors as he has been in the past and, if he is no longer to be found at the Municipal Council, he will be found even closer to the port, at the Medical Centre. As he has a fishing boat and knows the waters around the island very well, he has a lot of advice for potential visitors and strongly recommended that one should always anchor in Corvo with two anchors.

Weather fronts can approach very quickly and as they come from the west with absolutely no land in the way to slow them down, conditions can change almost instantaneously. The other danger around Corvo is that some of the offlying rocks have not been chartered accurately. A recent victim in May 1993 was a large Portuguese fishing vessel which ran onto a volcanic pinnacle some 500 metres from the northeast shore. The holed vessel foundered on a nearby beach and although the crew were saved, the boat itself could not be rescued.

Formalities

Boats are usually met by a marine police officer, whose office is at the Posto Maritimo, immediately above the harbour. He can also be seen meeting

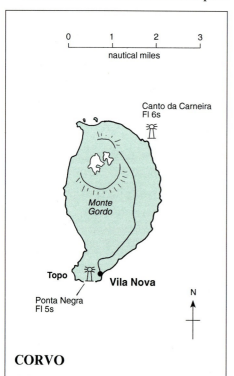

CORVO

Vila Nova

CORVO
SMALL IS BEAUTIFUL

Visit the smallest island in the Azores where time stands still and you can savour the untouched beauty of nature.

CÂMARA MUNICIPAL DO CORVO
9980 VILA NOVA, CORVO, AZORES

the small plane and is responsible for traffic, the island having some ten cars. There is a Guarda Fiscal office in a red roofed building on the hill overlooking the runway. The Posto Maritimo usually monitors VHF Channel 16 during daytime, as do the others who have VHF radios, amongst them the Municipal Council.

Port Facilities

The small quay in Porto da Casa in Vila Nova offers hardly any protection from the swell which rolls in relentlessly even in the calmest of weathers. Because of the constant surge it can be dangerous to come alongside the quay. It is better to anchor off and take the dinghy to the steps. The small headland offers some protection in north and northeast winds, while the wharf itself offers some protection in west or southwest winds, but only if the winds are light.

There are no facilities in the port, although a 30 ton crane has been brought in for the planned work on extending the present quay. The plan is to widen this to 8 metres and lengthen it to 32 metres, which should considerably increase protection in the small harbour. According to the municipal president, even if the planned work does not take place, the crane is there to stay and may come in handy should a yacht need its help in an emergency.

Shore Facilities

There are several small grocery shops, with a reasonable selection of basic staples, frozen foods and some fresh fruit and vegetables. Whatever there is has to be transported from Flores as very little is grown on Corvo itself. The opening hours are Monday to Friday 0900-1230, 1400-1800, Saturdays only in the morning. Bread must be ordered from one of the shops, as it is only baked for regular customers.

O Caldeirão, the only restaurant on the island, is close to the old harbour, Porto Novo, and the three windmills overlooking it. The restaurant belongs to the Municipal Council as does a jeep which can be hired for the obligatory trip to the crater in the centre of the island, which is highly recommended.

The post office and telephone counter is at the crossroads on Avenida Nova, open Monday to Friday 0900-1230, 1400-1800. Although there is no pharmacy on the island, in an emergency medicine can be obtained from the medical centre. Tel. 56153.

O BOQUEIRÃO

There are three alternative anchorages close to Vila Nova, the first is the O Boqueirão inlet, which has the old whaling ramp. There is a set of landing steps in the narrow inlet west of the ramp. The island's fuel station stands at the top of the ramp and fuel can be obtained from here in drums.

PORTO NOVO

Further west, about half a mile from Porto da Casa, is Porto Novo. This is in fact a misnomer, as this broken down port overlooked by a lighthouse and windmills is the oldest harbour on the island. The old quay, built of lava blocks, is now surrounded by shallow water, but would make a good landing place for a dinghy. If there is no swell, a yacht can be taken in quite close to the shore.

AREIA

Yet another anchorage is at Areia, close to the natural pools west of Porto Novo. The anchorage offers reasonable protection in east and northeast winds and there are some landings steps close to the end of the existing runway.

BAIA DO TOPO

In strong winds from northeast through east to southeast local boats seek protection in Topo Bay, north of Ponta do Topo, on the west side of the island. The ground is boulders interspersed with sandy patches and is overlooked by the old meteorological station due to be demolished and therefore no longer to be used as a reference point, although it still appears on Portuguese charts.

FLORES

This most westerly of the islands is usually the first to be sighted by transatlantic sailors.

Land ho! ... a mystic dome like a mountain of silver stood alone in the sea ahead. Although the land was completely hidden by the white, glistening haze that shone in the sun like polished silver, I felt sure that it was Flores Island.

So wrote Joshua Slocum over 100 years ago, and this misty phenomenon can still conceal the island today.

The discovery of Flores and neighbouring Corvo took place much later than the other islands, the two only being sighted in 1452 by the Portuguese navigator Diogo de Teive and his son. Settlement of the island did not become established for another fifty years. Due to its remoteness and lack of a good natural harbour, Flores remained isolated, with few ships calling to trade or provision, although it was still sacked by English privateers in the 16th century.

The building of an airport, improvement in port facilities and the opening of a French meteorological observatory and satellite tracking station in the 1960's decreased this isolation. The French base closed down in 1993, leaving the legacy that French is the most widely spoken foreign language by the islanders. Life today continues to revolve much as it always has done around an agricultural economy and the passing of the seasons.

The early settlers who named their island Flores, Isle of Flowers, had good cause and no island is truer to its name than Flores. Exotic flowers of all hues line the roadside in profusion. In many places the road is bordered by banks of rambling roses, large daisies, flaming red or speckled gold cannas and masses of the ubiquitous hydrangea. The island is lovely in the typical Azorean way of lakes and craters, rolling hills thick with vegetation and craggy cliffs along the coast. There is no doubt that Flores has the most spectacular scenery of any island in the Azores; perpendicular cliffs, waterfalls, rock arches, deep caves and rocky offshore islets. The Enxaréus Grotto on the east coast is an enormous cave 50 metres long and 25 metres wide.

It is worth hiring a car or taxi to spend a day driving around this floral island. As well as the flowers and the scenery, there are countless birds and lots of rabbits. In some places the rabbits are almost a traffic hazard as they lie sunning themselves in the middle of the road and then dashing for the nearest hedge with suicidal disdain.

The small harbour of the main town Santa Cruz can only be used in good weather. Many yachts arriving from across the Atlantic stop at this peaceful island until a change in the wind sends them scurrying for the safety of Horta 132 miles further east. With the improvements made recently to the port of Lajes, it is expected that many more will make the island of Flores their first stop in the Azores.

NAVIGATION

Much of the scenery of Flores can only be appreciated by boat. Even if one does not have time to stop and anchor, and provided the weather is quite settled, it is well worth trying to sail around the island. This can be accomplished in one day and gives one the opportunity to see sights which are denied those visiting the island by land. Some of the grottoes on the east coast are large enough to drive a boat in, although not recommended to those with a mast.

Although there are a number of offlying rocks around the island, most of them are close inshore and clearly visible. Sailing south from Santa Cruz clockwise around the island there are a number of anchorages on the southeast coast before one reaches the second largest settlement of the island at Lajes.

Sailing west from Lajes there are several day anchorages on the south and southwest coasts of the island. All the villages along this coast, such as Lajedo or Mosteiro, are set inland with no easy access from the sea. The coast is peppered with rocky islets lying close inshore but easily avoided in clear weather. There are several bays providing good shelter in northeast winds such as Fajãzinha and Fajã Grande.

Beyond Fajã Grande and Punta de Fajã the coast is inhospitable with high cliffs and no anchorages. The rocky islet Ilhéu Monchique stands proudly offshore, the westernmost point of Europe and, in the old days, a point of reference for westbound navigators.

On the northwest coast, past Ilhéu de Maria Vaz, a rocky islet close to the fishing hamlet of Pequeiro provides a perfect anchorage protected from the southwest by the islet itself. A short promontory provides additional protection by a rocky beach.

Built in 1911 the Albarnaz lighthouse on the northwest point of Flores is the most westernmost navigation aid in Europe. The lighthouse is open to visitors and the staff are very keen to show off their excellently maintained installation.

There are two anchorages close to the large village of Ponta Delgada on the northeast point of the island. Along the east coast there are wind acceleration zones in northeast winds. Sailing south along this coast, one place where one may be tempted to close with the forbidding shore is immediately to the north of Ilhéu de Alvaro Rodrigues, where the waves have carved a large grotto out of the cliffs. There is deep water right up to the entrance into the cave, which is about 10 metres high and 20 metres deep. The spot is renowned among divers for its sea bass. The rock formations along this coast are truly spectacular and there is enough depth to negotiate the narrow pass between Alvaro Rodrigues and the sheer cliff, but this is not for the faint hearted!

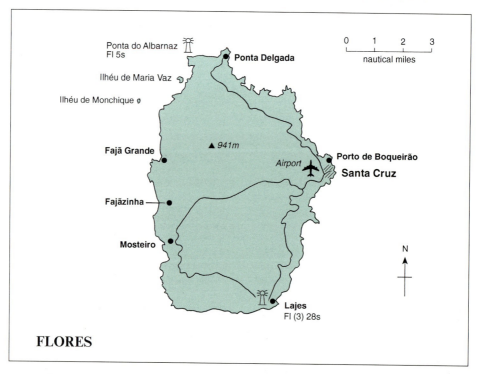

FLORES

LIGHTS

Santa Cruz - Porto Velho 39°27'.2N 31°07'.3W Fl G 5s 14m 4M
Porto das Poças 39°27'.0N 31°07'.4W Fl G 3s 9m 5M
Ponta das Lajes 39°22'.5N 31°10'.4W Fl(3) W 28s 90m 26M
Fajã Grande 39°27'.5N 31°15'.5W Fl W 5s 14m 4M
Ponta do Albarnaz 39°31'.1N 31°13'.9W Fl W 5s 87m 22M

SANTA CRUZ

The main town of Flores is small and pleasant with attractive houses and an imposing twin towered church in black and white Azorean style. Although relatively small, Santa Cruz has a surprisingly good selection of shops and also some of the most helpful people in the Azores.

Located in a traditional house is the Ethnographic Museum, which has an interesting collection of old furniture, domestic utensils and farming implements. The kitchen is particularly authentic. The museum is open Monday to Friday, 0900-1230, 1400-1730.

A large launch, which makes the twice weekly 13 mile trip to Corvo, normally lies alongside the main wharf. The launch, called *Familia Augusto*, is operated by José Augusto Junior, a prominent member of this local sailing dynasty, whose helpfulness is legendary. José is not only an excellent sailor, but also an accomplished diver and might be induced to part with valuable advice on the best diving and spearfishing spots on the island.

To the north of Porto das Poças is the old fishing harbour of Santa Cruz, which is not suitable for keeled boats, although it is still used by the local fishermen, whose boats are pulled ashore as soon as they land their catch. This harbour is overlooked by the old light and Customs still has its office there.

Porto das Poças

This harbour serving Santa Cruz should only be entered in settled weather. Swell and surge are a major problem and even in settled conditions there is always some surge in this small harbour protected from the east by a detached breakwater and from the other directions by several rocks. All rocks are clearly visible as seas break over them even in the calmest of weathers.

The Capitania should always be advised if one intends to come into Porto das Poças. They monitor VHF Channel 16 during office hours, Monday to Friday 0900-1730. Outside those hours, Channel 16 is usually monitored by some of the fishermen who have sets at home. If help or advice is needed, one should contact Radio Naval on Channel 16. If the operator does not speak English, one should try and get him to put a call through to the regional airline office (SATA), on 52425, where Antonio Francisco Melho will provide the necessary advice, as he has done on many occasions in the past.

Approaches

The red and white leading marks are clearly visible on the hill behind the port and should be lined up on 285°. Because of the constant swell and surge, the narrow pass between two sets of rocks should be negotiated with sufficient power. A right turn should be made as soon as the small harbour opens up to starboard. The few moorings should be avoided when manoeuvring and help may be needed to take at least two lines ashore to steady the boat. Normally it is possible to use at least one of the

Porto das Poças

moorings to keep off the breakwater. It is advisable to face south, so as to be able to leave quickly should the weather deteriorate. For this reason, one's own anchor should only be used as an additional precaution as it is safer to lie to lines taken to the outer breakwater.

As the outer breakwater is not connected to the shore, the dinghy should be taken to the main quay and landed by the steps, close to the crane. The 15 ton crane is used to haul out local fishing boats and lighters, but has been used on occasions to lift out visiting yachts when conditions inside the harbour have become threatening. Such a situation occurred in August 1990 when several yachts were moored in Porto das Poças. As an unusually deep depression starting forming west of Faial, the locals advised the yacht owners to leave the harbour as they would be safer at sea. Only some skippers took this advice and when 60 knot winds and huge waves crashed into the port, the locals made superhuman efforts to save the remaining yachts, which they managed to crane onto the main wharf.

Formalities

All three authorities should be visited in turn. Customs has an office in the old fishing harbour, while the Capitania is located in a large building in Rua Senador André Freitas, Tel. 52437, the main street of Santa Cruz leading from the old harbour into the centre. The Guarda Fiscal is located in the main square, at the top of the same street.

An official from the Capitania will probably meet the yacht on arrival. The authorities should be informed in advance of one's cruising plans, especially if one plans on stopping in some of the anchorages around the island. As one may be forced to leave the port in a hurry, should the weather change unexpectedly, the Capitania should be told of one's contingency plan, which is either to sail to Lajes and seek shelter there, or if the winds are from northeast or east, to Fajã Grande on the other side of the island.

Port Facilities

There is a water tap at the top of the ramp, but otherwise the harbour is very basic. There is no fuel in the port and it has to be carried in jerrycans from the fuel station on Rua Senador Freitas.

Marine Services

Castanheira & Soares, a company whose workshop is located in the industrial estate behind the old whaling station will undertake work on diesel engines, some electrical repair as well as welding and metalwork. Although working mainly on cars and trucks, their mechanics are the most skilled on the island and also undertake work on local fishing boats.

José Augusto Junior, who runs the *Familia Augusto*, is a skilled diesel mechanic and although he normally works only on his own boats, he may be persuaded to help out in a serious emergency. Tel. 52289.

Movipesca, Rua Diogo Chagas, the only chandlery, has a small selection of nautical equipment, some hardware, tools, fishing and diving gear. Monday to Friday 0830-1200, 1330-1800.

Shore Facilities
Provisioning

The fresh vegetable and fruit selection is rather disappointing on such a verdant island, but this is because, with the exception of a few seasonal things, most fruit is brought out from Portugal by a ship calling on average once a month.

Centro Comercial Boaventura Ramos, Rua Senator André Freitas 6, Tel. 52656, is a supermarket with a good selection of food products, including fresh vegetables, cheeses and meat. Open Monday to Friday 0815-1200, 1330-1730, Saturday 0845-1300.

A smaller supermarket is Minimercado Germano de Deus, in Praça Marques de Pombal, open Monday to Friday 0830-1230, 1330-1900, Saturday 0830-1300.

Another minimarket is in Rua Diogo Chagas, open Monday to Friday, 0900-

1830, Saturday 0900-1300.

Also in Rua Senador Freitas is the only bakery, Padaria Belmiro Silva, selling tasty fresh bread and rolls, as well as pastries and sandwiches.

Lourenço & Lourenço, Tel. 52144, a wholesaler in the industrial estate by the old whaling station, sells beer, soft drinks and tinned goods.

Communications

The post office is in Rua Senador André Freitas, open Monday to Friday, 0900-1230, 1400-1800. Metered telephone calls can be made from there and faxes sent and received (Fax 52577). Phonecards are also on sale and there is a cardphone in the main square, Praça Marques de Pombal.

There is a taxi rank in the main square (Tel. 52376). Buses connect the capital with the other main settlements on the island, but the service is not too frequent. The bus stop is in the central car park, near the pharmacy and medical centre.

Car hire

Auto Turistica Flores, at Residencial Flores, Travessa de São José 3, opposite the post office, Tel. 52190, Fax 52621.

Ocidental Rent-a-Car, at Hotel Ocidental, near the airport, Tel. 52142, 52351, Fax 52119.

Medical

Health Centre, Praça 25 Abril, Santa Cruz, Tel. 52316.

Restaurants

The nearest restaurant to the port is Lita, Travessa de Alfandega 4, Tel. 52299, opposite the customs house in the old harbour. Their speciality are the *cataplana* dishes, meals cooked in a round dish like a wok with a lid, which allows the two parts to be sealed so that the food is baked in its own steam and juices. Among some of the tasty dishes cooked this way are stewed pork with cockles, salted cod or mixed seafood.

For a square meal one should make the kilometre walk to the Hotel Ocidental, near the old whaling station, on the outskirts of Santa Cruz. Dinner is served between 2000 and 2130 and has to be booked in advance (Tel. 52142). The prices are very reasonable and the hotel has its own courtesy minibus.

The cheapest meals not only on Flores but perhaps anywhere in the Azores, can be had at the Castanheira & Soares self-service restaurant in the industrial estate behind the old whaling station. The restaurant caters mainly for workers and fishermen and is open both for lunch and dinner.

Also overlooking the old whaling station is the aptly called Restaurante Baleia, Tel. 52462, serving local specialities, mainly freshly caught fish.

EAST COAST

Only one mile south of Santa Cruz, at Fajã de Conde, there is a pleasant anchorage with sandy patches providing good protection even in northerly winds. One can anchor in 10 metres south of the village of Caveira and land on the black sandy beach. Further south, there is another good anchorage at Fajã Pedro

AUTO TURÍSTICA FLORES, LDA.

rent-a-car

☎ 52190 – FAX 52621
9970 SANTA CRUZ DAS FLORES

Viero, in the lee of Ponta Caveira, on whose north side stands an impressive sea grotto. The cave is large enough for the local boats to turn around in and, in settled weather, can be explored at leisure in a dinghy.

LAJES

One of several villages in the Azores having this name, the one on Flores should be referred to as Lajes das Flores to avoid confusion. After considerable political debate and local controversy, Lajes won the argument to have the major port of the island built there. Financed by the Regional Government and the European Community, the extended breakwater and vastly improved port installation will almost turn Lajes into an all-weather port and will thus provide a much needed, and at the same time, safe and convenient port of entry into the Azores. There is no doubt that starting in 1994, when work in the port is expected to be completed, many yachts arriving from the west will make their entry into the Azores in Flores rather than carry on to one of the traditional ports further east. This will make a lot of sense and will also give visiting sailors the opportunity to acquaint themselves sooner with the many attractions of the archipelago.

The village of Lajes boasts the biggest fiesta on the island, a local extravaganza lasting several days and held during the last weekend of July. The Feast of the Emigrant brings back many locals or their descendants, who have made their fortunes overseas, mainly in the USA and Canada, but also from mainland Portugal. The fiesta attracts artists from other Azorean islands as well as former Portuguese colonies. There are folk, pop and brass band concerts, sporting events, culinary exhibitions and much more. Details of future events can be obtained from José Maria Silva, Camara Municipal, 9960 Lajes das Flores.

Formalities

Although Lajes has not yet been designated an official port of entry, yachts arriving from overseas are allowed to call there first. It is expected that by 1994, when work in the port will have been completed, both the Guarda Fiscal and Capitania will have their own offices in Lajes. For the time being, only the former has an office in Lajes. To obtain the Transit Log, one must visit the Capitania in Santa Cruz, which can be reached either by bus or taxi. The bus leaves in the morning and returns in the afternoon, but there is no service on Tuesdays and Thursdays. A round trip by taxi costs 2000 escudos, which is approximately 12 US dollars.

Port Facilities

With only one commercial ship expected once every three weeks and, so far, a very small local fishing fleet, visiting yachts can be assured of finding space alongside the quay. The only time when more fishing boats are expected is during the tuna season, from mid-July to the end of August.

The prevailing winds are from the south southwest, so the port was built to provide protection from that direction, but even in northeast winds the swell is negligible. If there is too much movement and one cannot come alongside, one should anchor inside the port and take the dinghy to the last set of steps, by the beach. The main wharf is reserved for larger commercial vessels, whereas the inner quays should be used by smaller fishing vessels and yachts. The most convenient for the latter is the smaller 30 metre long quay on the west side of the post, by the beach. Having been built primarily for larger vessels, the quay is rather high, so yachts should be careful when coming alongside. Four metal steps are set into the quay making it easier to climb up from a yacht.

There are plans to have a fuel station on the quay, but in the meantime fuel has to be brought down in trucks from the village in drums or jerrycans. A toilet and shower block is also planned in the harbour. The harbour crane can lift up to 15 tons.

LAJES
FLORES

The most westerly port in Europe invites you to make your first landfall in the flower garden of the Azores.

CÂMARA MUNICIPAL DAS LAJES DAS FLORES
TEL: (092) 53650 — FAX: (092) 53444

Lajes

Marine Services

For emergency repairs it is best to contact Honorato Gonçalves de Freitas who is in charge of the municipal workshop located on the road leading from the harbour into the village. He is not only a skilled diesel mechanic, but also is a keen diver, can handle sail repairs and also will undertake welding as he has all the necessary equipment.

A hardware and grocery store, which has some chandlery items, belongs to João Germano de Deus, who also runs the only fuel station, which is right outside his shop. He also sells gas (LPG) and will deliver both groceries and fuel to yachts. One of his partners, André Rodas, is vice-commodore of the yacht club, temporarily located in a container in the port. André is a good local contact, who has helped several visiting sailors in the past and is keen to attract more yachts to Lajes.

Shore Facilities

The village has three minimarkets with a reasonable selection of basic staples as well as fresh meat, vegetables, local cheeses and freshly baked bread. The best stocked is Supermercado Flor Peixe, above the lighthouse, open Monday to Friday 0900-1230, 1330-1800, Saturday 0900-1300. Another minimarket is that of João Germano de Deus mentioned above for his chandlery.

On the road leading up from the harbour is a small grocery and restaurant, Loja da Senhora Teresa Salgado, who will cook a meal if asked. If needed, bread can also be ordered from Senhora Teresa. Further along is another small bar and restaurant, Beira Mar, specialising in fish dishes.

The bus stop is by the roundabout below the Municipal Council, where one will also find the only public telephone. The small post office is next to the church.

FAJÃZINHA

When sailing west from Lajes, the first village which can be reached from the sea is Fajãzinha lying at the head of a wide bay protected from north through east to south. The bay is fronted by a rocky beach with several sandy spots with 4 to 5 metres depth where one can anchor quite close to the beach. A half kilometre walk along a steep path leads into the small village where a couple of houses proudly display shields showing that they were built in the 1860s. Most houses are only lived in during the summer and even the two small shops and cafés in the tiny square below the church only open at the height of the summer season. A good time to visit is during the feast dedicated to the local patron saint, Nossa Senhora dos Remedios, on the first weekend in July.

FAJÃ GRANDE

The largest village on the west coast has a good landing at a quay by the old slipway, immediately to the north of the light. The quay has seen better days and the only place where one can come alongside with a keeled boat at high water, with depth of at least 2 metres, is on the east side of the quay by the steps and diving board. Otherwise it is better to anchor in 4 metres close to the quay and perhaps take a line ashore, although unfortunately there is nothing to tie it to. The local swimming pool, a low white building close to the quay, has public showers as well as a small café.

The wide beach and harbour are overlooked by high cliffs with several waterfalls plunging hundreds of metres to sea level. It is a tranquil spot and an excellent anchorage in northeast or east winds. To the south of the bay, the black lava rock foreshore is broken up by several deep inlets. In settled weather the second inlet south of the lighthouse is deep enough to anchor in.

There are only two small grocery shops in Fajã Grande. The larger one, halfway up the main street close to the church, belongs to Antonio Pureza Ramos. This also doubles up as a café and restaurant, which will serve a meal if ordered in advance. A little further up past the church is the bus stop to Santa Cruz.

PONTA DELGADA

There are two anchorages close to this large village on the northeast point of the island. In northeast winds, the anchorage northwest of Ponta Delgada in the lee of João Martin islet is free of swell. There are some shallow patches between the offlying islet and the shore, so the bay should be entered from the west. One can anchor in 5 metres close to the rocky beach, although the ground is made up of large boulders which may foul the anchor. A flight of concrete steps leads up the steep cliff to the village. This attractive and relatively safe anchorage in settled weather offers good protection in winds from northeast to southwest. It is a popular fishing spot.

The second anchorage, in the bay south of Ponta Delgada, where local fishermen keep their boat, has a short breakwater and slipway. There are about ten boats pulled up on the concrete ramp, as there is always some swell except in southwest winds when either of the two bays can be used. The dinghy can be left by the steps at the bottom of the slipway. A half kilometre walk takes one into the village, which has a couple of small shops.

SÃO PEDRO

A good anchorage in southwest winds north of the old whaling station at Porto do Boqueirão. There are rocks to be avoided when entering the bay, both to the north (Baixa Vermelha) and to the east, off Ponta São Pedro, all of which are visible in good light. The anchorage offers the best protection in the vicinity of Santa Cruz.

PORTO DE BOQUEIRÃO

The narrow bay leading to the old ramp, where whales used to be hauled ashore, is fringed by several large rocks. The dinghy can be landed at the steps leading up to the old wharf. An industrial estate has sprung up behind the old whaling station, with workshops and a couple of restaurants. It is a kilometre walk into Santa Cruz.

São Pedro

LIST OF CHARTS

BRITISH ADMIRALTY

		Scale
1950	The Azores Archipelago	1,000,000
1946	Flores and Corvo	150,000
	Santa Cruz das Flores, Lajes das Flores, Vila Nova (Corvo)	25,000
1956	Azores Central Group	175,000
1957	Harbours in Central Group	
	Horta, Vila da Praia (Graciosa), Praia da Vitória (Terceira), Angra do Heroísmo (Terceira), Canal do Faial	10,000
1958	Ilha de São Miguel	150,000
	Ponta Delgada	12,000
	Vila Franca do Campo, Capelas	25,000
1865	Santa Maria and Formigas Islands	150,000
	Vila do Porto (Santa Maria), São Lourenço (Santa Maria)	12,000

US DEFENCE MAPPING AGENCY

51002	The Azores Archipelago	750,000
51041	Flores and Corvo	250,000
	Santa Cruz das Flores, Lajes das Flores	20,000
51061	Faial, Graciosa, Terceira, Pico and São Jorge	250,000
51062	Canal of Faial	25,000
	Santa Cruz de Graciosa, Angra do Heroísmo (Terceira)	15,000
	Praia da Vitória (Terceira)	7,500
51064	Eastern Approaches to Terceira	25,000
51081	São Miguel and Santa Maria	250,000
	Vila Franca do Campo	20,000
	Vila do Porto	10,000
51082	Ponta Delgada (São Miguel)	7,500

AERO RADIO BEACONS

Santa Maria	SMA	323kHz	300miles	36°59'75N	25°10'57W
Santa Maria	STA	240kHz	200miles	36°56'90N	25°10'00W
Ponta Delgada (S. Miguel)	MGL	371kHz	200miles	37°44'43N	25°35'07W
Ponta Delgada (S. Miguel)	PD	351kHz	25miles	37°44'05N	25°40'53W
Lajes (Terceira)	GP	341kHz	50miles	38°46'98N	27°06'85W
Graciosa	GRA	283kHz	100miles	39°05'00N	28°01'00W
Horta (Faial)	FIL	380kHz	250miles	38°31'33N	28°41'25W
Horta (Faial)	HT	360kHz	25miles	38°31'18N	28°37'80W
Flores	FLO	270kHz	250miles	39°26'63N	31°0980W

All of the above radio beacons are operational 24 hours on A2A transmission mode